# Mental Toughness Tips

## For Roller Derby and Beyond

Naomi Sweetart Weitz

Copyright © 2018 Naomi Sweetart Weitz

Cover Photo by Emily Violent Ems Nichols
Cover and interior graphic design by Skyler Weitz
Drawings by Paul Gregg
Stick figures by Naomi Sweetart Weitz
Thank you to my editors: Allyson Ally Oops Coit, Sydney Octopow Lindgren, Macie Wombpunch Stead, and Jess Crashtastrophe Haberman

All rights reserved.

No part of this book may be reproduced in any form or by any electronic or mechanical means including photo copying, scanning, or by any information storage and retrieval system without express written permission from the author.

This book is not intended as a substitute for the medical advice of a licensed physician. The reader should consult with their doctor in any matters relating to their health. The content of this book is intended for educational and entertainment purposes only and is not intended or considered to be professional counseling or advice, nor should it be considered any type of professional counseling transaction. Psychological services of any nature should be sought directly from a licensed professional. Not all exercise is suitable for every individual. To reduce the risk of injury, consult your doctor before completing any of the activities in this book. This book is made available without any warranties or guarantees of any kind and the author and contributors disclaim any liability, loss or damage, resulting from its use.

ISBN: 1727557743

ISBN-13: 9781727557749

## DEDICATION

This book is dedicated to my team,

Spokannibals Roller Derby.

# CONTENTS

- ☐ Introduction — 2
- ☐ Celebrate Nice Falls — 18
- ☐ Get The Right Ingredients For Success — 19
- ☐ Stretch Out Of Your Comfort Zone — 20
- ☐ Be Calm: 4-7-8 Breathing — 21
- ☐ Focus On Your Focus — 22
- ☐ Know The Benefits Of Stress — 23
- ☐ Tap Into Your Strengths — 24
- ☐ Pace Yourself — 26
- ☐ Be Connected: Feel The Pulse — 28
- ☐ Maximize Your Commitment — 29
- ☐ Be Value-Driven — 32
- ☐ Be In Control: Woodchopper — 34
- ☐ Take Calculated Risks — 35
- ☐ Practice And Play With Intention — 36
- ☐ Create Space — 38
- ☐ Don't Choke — 40
- ☐ Form New Habits — 42
- ☐ Get In The Green Zone — 45
- ☐ Win Ugly — 48
- ☐ Be Shining: Star Pose — 49
- ☐ Keep Your Head In The Game When Your Team Is Down — 50
- ☐ Stay Hydrated — 52
- ☐ Be Self-Aware: Mental Toughness Quiz — 54
- ☐ Keep Your Power — 56
- ☐ Set Short-Term Goals — 58
- ☐ Be Remembered: Create Your Own Legacy — 60

| | |
|---|---|
| ☐ Crush Cliques | 62 |
| ☐ Achieve A State Of Coherence | 63 |
| ☐ Be Focused: Experience Your Focusing And Defocusing Networks | 66 |
| ☐ Have Just The Right Amount Of Confidence | 68 |
| ☐ Double Your Happiness | 70 |
| ☐ Be Mindful: Breath Counting | 71 |
| ☐ Don't Sweat The Small Stuff | 72 |
| ☐ Ride The Fear | 74 |
| ☐ Challenge Self-Doubts | 76 |
| ☐ Give Great Feedback | 78 |
| ☐ Put On The Pressure | 80 |
| ☐ Be Connected: Triangle Pose | 82 |
| ☐ Be Energized: Outer Qi Shower | 83 |
| ☐ Be The Lion, Not The Dog | 84 |
| ☐ Be Trusting: Relationship Exercises | 86 |
| ☐ Know The Difference Between Discomfort and Pain | 87 |
| ☐ Have A Positive Attitude | 88 |
| ☐ Be Focused: Focus Training Exercise I | 90 |
| ☐ Meet Yourself Where You're At | 97 |
| ☐ Flip Negative Thinking | 98 |
| ☐ Give Everyone A Role | 100 |
| ☐ Know How To Resolve Conflicts | 102 |
| ☐ Be Mindful: Basic Mindfulness Exercise | 104 |
| ☐ Feedback Is Your Friend | 106 |
| ☐ Awaken Your Senses | 108 |
| ☐ Recognize Your Well Dones | 109 |
| ☐ Be Flexible: Half Lord Of The Fishes Pose | 110 |
| ☐ Practice Tapas | 112 |

| | |
|---|---|
| ☐ Come Back Strong After An Injury | 113 |
| ☐ Use The Power Of "Yet" | 118 |
| ☐ Honor All Emotions | 120 |
| ☐ Be Positive: Put Your Derby Name Into Action | 122 |
| ☐ Maximize Your Chances Of Being In The Zone | 124 |
| ☐ Take Concussions Seriously | 125 |
| ☐ Defuse From Your Thoughts | 129 |
| ☐ Know Perfection Is A Myth | 132 |
| ☐ Be Driven: Goal Mapping | 133 |
| ☐ Be Your Best Self | 139 |
| ☐ Practice Radical Acceptance | 140 |
| ☐ Win With Class, Lose With Grace | 142 |
| ☐ Be Mindful: Roller Derby Mindfulness Activity I | 144 |
| ☐ Take Care Of Yourself | 145 |
| ☐ Approach Not Avoid | 146 |
| ☐ Promote Healthy Body Images | 148 |
| ☐ Soften Your Edges | 150 |
| ☐ Be Whole: Identify Which Emotions Are Barriers To Your Performance | 152 |
| ☐ Transform By Doing | 153 |
| ☐ Be Aggressive | 154 |
| ☐ Be Focused: Make A Distraction Plan | 156 |
| ☐ Respect Karma | 158 |
| ☐ Develop Your Quiet Eye | 160 |
| ☐ Use Your Supports | 162 |
| ☐ Be Focused: Eagle Pose | 164 |
| ☐ Be Cognitively Flexible | 166 |
| ☐ Make It OK To Make Mistakes | 167 |
| ☐ Feel Your Emotions | 168 |
| ☐ Send And Receive The Right Message | 170 |

| | |
|---|---|
| ☐ Be In Control: Chill Out | 172 |
| ☐ Namaste | 174 |
| ☐ Be Focused: Lion's Breath | 175 |
| ☐ Be Self-Aware: Mountain Pose | 176 |
| ☐ Be Centered: 5-4-3-2-1 Centering Exercise | 177 |
| ☐ Give Up Attachment To Outcomes | 178 |
| ☐ Plan For Retirement | 180 |
| ☐ Beware Of The SHOULDS | 182 |
| ☐ Develop the Vividness Of Your Imagery | 184 |
| ☐ Be Your Best Self: 14-Day Character Building Challenge | 186 |
| ☐ Use Willpower | 187 |
| ☐ Be Here Now | 188 |
| ☐ Imagine Yourself As Your Hero | 190 |
| ☐ Focus On Results | 192 |
| ☐ Keep Emotional Tanks Filled | 194 |
| ☐ Create A Positive Practice Space | 197 |
| ☐ Use Your Wise Mind | 198 |
| ☐ Tolerate Distress | 200 |
| ☐ Be Strong: Guided Meditation For Finding Your Strengths And Abilities | 202 |
| ☐ Be Balanced: Tune Up Your Chakras | 204 |
| ☐ Improve Your Visual Focus | 207 |
| ☐ Optimize Your Field Of Awareness | 208 |
| ☐ Stabilize Your Confidence | 210 |
| ☐ Be Attentive: Improve Your Memory | 212 |
| ☐ Find Unity | 213 |
| ☐ Harness The Power Of Positive Thought | 214 |
| ☐ Be Balanced: Tree Pose | 216 |
| ☐ Find Your Purpose | 218 |

| | |
|---|---|
| ☐ Focus On What You Can Control | 220 |
| ☐ Learn To Reset And Let Go | 222 |
| ☐ Don't Be Sorry | 223 |
| ☐ Cool Off Before Confronting Teammates | 224 |
| ☐ Be Present: Listen | 226 |
| ☐ Be Supportive: Got Your Back | 227 |
| ☐ Acknowledge Your Supports | 228 |
| ☐ Welcome Your Emotions | 230 |
| ☐ Set S.M.A.R.T. Goals | 232 |
| ☐ Be Inspired: Live By Your Motto | 234 |
| ☐ Prevent Focus Failure | 236 |
| ☐ Improve Auditory Focus | 238 |
| ☐ Be Calm: Progressive Muscle Relaxation | 239 |
| ☐ Find Your Fight Song | 242 |
| ☐ Give The Other Team Their Win | 243 |
| ☐ Welcome Opposites Of Thought | 244 |
| ☐ Fake It 'Til You Make It | 246 |
| ☐ Be Mindful: Mindfulness Quiz | 248 |
| ☐ Focus On Solutions | 251 |
| ☐ Recognize Indirect Emotions | 252 |
| ☐ Commit To Your Values | 254 |
| ☐ Take A Yogic Power Nap | 256 |
| ☐ Be Confident: Plank Pose | 258 |
| ☐ Be Focused: Scanning And Recognition | 260 |
| ☐ Use Imagery For Self-Awareness | 262 |
| ☐ Be Calm: Warming Body Scan | 265 |
| ☐ Create Change | 266 |
| ☐ Be Courageous: Climb A Fear Ladder | 268 |
| ☐ Assess Your Team's Culture | 270 |
| ☐ Prevent Burnout | 273 |

- ☐ Expect The Unexpected — 276
- ☐ Develop A Healthy Attitude Toward Competition — 278
- ☐ Train Your Vision To Reduce Concussion — 281
- ☐ Plan For Poise — 282
- ☐ Calibrate Your Sense Of Proprioception — 285
- ☐ Be Fired Up: Breath Of Fire — 286
- ☐ Know Your Triggers — 288
- ☐ Be Strong: Warrior II Pose — 290
- ☐ Practice How You Play — 292
- ☐ Survive And Thrive In Your First Game — 294
- ☐ Be Powerful: Cobra Pose — 295
- ☐ Be Driven: My Dream Goal Exercise — 296
- ☐ Change Your Story — 298
- ☐ Train Like A Woman — 301
- ☐ Tame The Envy — 306
- ☐ Don't Make Excuses — 308
- ☐ Be Your Own Cheerleader — 310
- ☐ Avoid Unhelpful Thinking Styles — 312
- ☐ Find Strength While Injured — 314
- ☐ Be Poised: Inoculate Yourself Against Stress — 316
- ☐ Turn Your Weaknesses Into Strengths — 318
- ☐ Know When To Say When — 320
- ☐ Bridge The Gap Between Practice And Play — 322
- ☐ Be Focused: Focus Training Exercise II — 324
- ☐ Manage Your Emotions — 326
- ☐ Be Prepared: Create A Winning Routine — 328
- ☐ Be Centered: Still Water Guided Meditation — 330
- ☐ Grow Positive Seeds — 331
- ☐ Give Yourself Affirmations — 332

| | |
|---|---|
| ☐ Act On Impulse | 334 |
| ☐ Use Imagery To Correct Mistakes | 335 |
| ☐ Be Focused: Pass The Star | 336 |
| ☐ Be Courageous: Risk Taking Challenge | 337 |
| ☐ Prevent Burnout With The Four A's | 338 |
| ☐ Beware Of The Self-Fulfilling Prophecy | 339 |
| ☐ Improve Your Attentional Focus | 341 |
| ☐ Learn To Love Drills | 344 |
| ☐ Be Rested: Child Pose | 345 |
| ☐ See Challenges As Opportunities | 346 |
| ☐ Be Powerful: Be Your Own Superhero | 348 |
| ☐ Tone Your Vagus Nerve | 350 |
| ☐ Use The ABC's To Decrease Anxiety | 353 |
| ☐ Have Pride | 354 |
| ☐ Be United: Make A Forest | 355 |
| ☐ Fuel Your Brain | 356 |
| ☐ Fill Your Mind With Positive Imagery | 358 |
| ☐ Be Mindful: Roller Derby Mindfulness Activity II | 361 |
| ☐ Be A Risk Taker | 362 |
| ☐ Build An Internal Locus Of Control | 364 |
| ☐ Connect Goals, Actions, and Values | 366 |
| ☐ Take Advantage Of Being Hot | 369 |
| ☐ Take Credit Where Credit Is Due | 370 |
| ☐ Lose The Ego | 372 |
| ☐ Be Committed: Bow Pose | 373 |
| ☐ Take Opposite Actions | 374 |
| ☐ Pull Your Weight | 376 |
| ☐ Be Resilient In The Face Of Adversity | 378 |
| ☐ Deal With Disappointment | 380 |

- ☐ Achieve Your Goals With Confidence — 382
- ☐ Enjoy The Rush — 384
- ☐ Be Positive: Guided Meditation For Happiness — 386
- ☐ Burn The Boats — 388
- ☐ Savor The Peaks — 389
- ☐ Appendix — 391
- ☐ References — 407
- ☐ About The Author — 420

*The only thing standing between success and failure is mental toughness.*

## INTRODUCTION

Welcome to *Mental Toughness Tips for Roller Derby And Beyond*. This book has over 200 mental toughness tips and tools to help you become the very best skater, team member, and human you can possibly be. The tips provide information that can be applied to practices, games, and overall personal empowerment. The tools are techniques and exercises that will enhance your mental toughness skills.

Included here are useful facts, theories, and information as well as guided meditations, worksheets, physical yoga postures, mindfulness exercises, art activities, and lots more for both individuals and teams. Information is presented from differing approaches and viewpoints. There is something for everyone in this book so take what you need.

*Mental Toughness Tips For Roller Derby And Beyond* can help you:
- Optimize performance
- Improve focus
- Decrease anxiety
- Build character
- Manage emotions

- Be a great teammate
- Achieve goals
- Enjoy roller derby
- Fulfill your potential

This book includes material from the author's previous two books, *The Ultimate Mental Toughness Guide: Roller Derby* and *The Ultimate Mental Toughness Guide: Junior Roller Derby* plus lots of new information. This mental toughness book is for all ages, genders, and skill levels.

## Sports Psychology

Sports psychology uses psychological concepts to improve sports performance. Psychology is the study of the mind and how the mind influences emotions and behavior. Using sports psychology methods will lead to mental toughness.

This book talks a lot about performance. Performance is all that you do in roller derby. It is blocking, jamming, pivoting, being confident, having great character, being a great teammate, and more. Having a successful performance means doing what you do with excellence.

Mental toughness training should supplement your physical training and be approached in the same way. How an athlete performs is based on at least 60% psychological or mental factors. Some experts say mental toughness skills are everything.

The mental toughness information included here takes a holistic, mind-body approach to mental toughness. This means this book will help you transform the way your mind thinks so you can feel and do better. The "mind" part of the approach is cognitive and rational in nature. Also included are tips that will help you address what is going on in your body, particularly your central nervous system. By taking this "whole-brain" approach to mental toughness, you will maximize opportunities to improve your performance.

A lack of mental toughness can cause you to give up, give in, or give less. *Mental Toughness Tips For Roller Derby And Beyond* will help you be a successful athlete. The ideal profile includes the following characteristics:

- Highly self-confident
- Expects success
- Able to feel energized yet relaxed
- Feels in control
- Able to focus on the task at hand
- Sees difficult situations as exciting and challenging
- Has high standards but is flexible enough to learn from mistakes
- Has a positive attitude about performing
- Is determined and committed

The tips and tools included here come from Cognitive Behavioral Therapy, Acceptance and Commitment Therapy, Dialectical Behavior Therapy, mindfulness, neuroscience, studies on resilience, yoga, Zen practice, and more.

## Mental Toughness

Toughness, or strength, applies to the realms of our heart, mind, and body. Strength in our body has to do with the physical strength of our muscles, endurance, power, and how well our systems are functioning.

Strength in our mind involves cognitive strength. Having this means we can deal with distractions, sustain our focus on what is relevant, and have flexible thinking. Having strength in our heart means we have the emotional strength to manage our feelings, control our behaviors, and respond in a purposeful way. These three realms interact and influence one another.

Mental toughness means being able to function at our peak—to be at our very best. It is learning how to use the power of the mind to become stronger. Mental toughness means overcoming the emotional and cognitive barriers to our best performance. Ultimately, our mental toughness allows us to have the level of self-control needed to achieve our full potential.

Working on your mental toughness is like doing pushups for your mind. Just like building up physical muscles, building mental strength takes time and practice. Be patient, dedicated, and remember that achieving mental toughness is a lifelong journey, not a destination.

## How To Use This Book

You can read these mental toughness tips and tools in any order you want. Each skill can stand on its own. There are checkboxes next to each item in the Contents, allowing you to track your progress.

To get the most out of this book:
1. Put the tips into action. These tips will only help you if you take them off the page and out into your life.
2. Practice the tools and complete the activities and challenges. This will give you opportunities to expand and integrate your learning.
3. Revisit the tips over time. You will see things from a different perspective when you bring new experiences and wisdom to the table.

4. Share the tips with a friend. When we teach something to someone else, our own learning solidifies.

5. Record the meditations and imagery scripts. Record yourself or someone else saying the scripts out loud. This will let you completely relax and listen to the cues without having to read at the same time.

## Cognitive Behavioral Therapy

Cognitive Behavioral Therapy (CBT) is one of the most widely researched methods of change in psychology. This modality involves identifying and changing unhelpful or irrational thoughts to ones that are more helpful or rational. The "CBT Triangle" below demonstrates the core concept of this approach—that our thoughts, feelings, and actions are all interconnected. Essentially, when we can change our thinking, we can change the way we feel and how we live.

CBT developed to treat specific phobias, making *exposure,* or approaching that which we fear, another element of this treatment. Exposure helps individuals confront situations either *imaginally* or *in vivo* (in real life) so that their fear response subsides.

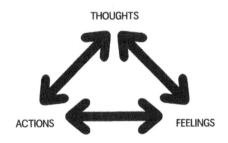

## Acceptance and Commitment Therapy

Acceptance and Commitment Therapy (ACT) uses mindfulness skills to help individuals live and behave in ways consistent with personal values while developing psychological flexibility. Identifying values (what is important to you) and living in a way that honors those values, despite how you are thinking or feeling, is a fundamental aspect of ACT.

Acceptance of things as they come, without evaluating or attempting to change them, is a skill developed through mindfulness exercises. ACT does not attempt to directly change or stop unwanted thoughts or feelings (as Cognitive Behavioral Therapy does) but instead encourages people to develop a new and compassionate relationship with those experiences. This shift can free people from difficulties attempting to control their experiences and help them become more open to actions consistent with their values.

## Dialectical Behavior Therapy

Dialectical Behavior Therapy (DBT) is a cognitive behavioral treatment developed by Dr. Marsha Linehan. DBT helps people learn and use new skills and strategies to develop a life that they experience as worth living. DBT skills include mindfulness, emotion regulation, distress tolerance, and interpersonal effectiveness. DBT was originally developed to treat those with chronic suicidal or self-harm behaviors.

## Neuroscience, Mindfulness, and Focused Breathing

Understanding how our brain works is necessary for building mental toughness. Consider the brain as having an upstairs and a downstairs. Our "upstairs brain," especially the Prefrontal Cortex (PFC), can be thought of as our rational brain. It is involved in planning, impulse control, social behavior, reason and language.

Our "downstairs brain" includes our limbic system and brain stem. Part of the limbic system, the amygdala, is involved in emotion, the consolidation of emotion-laded memories, anger, aggression, hunger, and pleasure. This is the part of the brain that prepares us for fight or flight mode—our autonomic stress response system. Our brain stem controls largely involuntary, vital functions such as heart rate, breathing, and body temperature.

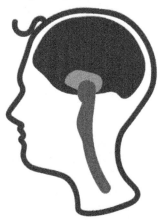

When our alarm system is triggered, our downstairs brain takes over. It partially shuts down our higher brain and prepares us to run, fight, or freeze. Danger signals are sent to the amygdala which determines whether input is life threatening by associating it with past experiences. The same danger signals are also sent to our frontal lobes which applies conscious awareness that can put the brakes on the stress response. Since the amygdala receives the danger signals first, our stress response system is already set into motion by the time it reaches our conscious awareness.

As an illustration of how this works, think about driving down the road when suddenly a deer leaps in front of your car. You can't take the time to work out what is happening and how you are going to respond, you just need to react. This is what our stress response system is designed for. It works great for those times when we need to let instinct take over for survival.

The stress response system is a very primitive part of our brain. It responds the same way to emotional or physical danger and has not evolved to be able to deal with the complex social and emotional situations humans encounter. And since our stress response system bases its information on images from past experiences, it is often wrong about the present reality. This causes us to be "hijacked" by our limbic system. Understanding your brain can put your emotional responses in a more helpful context.

Have you ever been on a hike and jumped to safety because you saw a snake? Did it ever turnout to be just a piece of rope? In that moment, without making a conscious decision about it, your flight or fight stress response system was activated. Your heart rate and breathing became rapid; your muscles tensed up; your pupils dilated to allow you to be more aware and observant of your surroundings; your skin may have appeared pale as blood rushed to your legs, arms, and brain. Your body just prepared itself to react to danger that was only psychological. It didn't really exist. It takes awareness to put the brakes on reactions and allow our upstairs, thinking, rational brain the time to see what is really going on.

When we apply this knowledge to roller derby, we discover we don't necessarily need to react to our body's alarm bells. When we experience strong, debilitating or destructive emotions such as fear or anger, we can learn to press the pause button on our reactions, assess the situation rationally, and then decide what we want to do. Mindfulness practice enhances our ability to do this by strengthening the thinking part of our brain, the Prefrontal Cortex.

Other benefits of mindfulness practice include:
- Increases in self-awareness and self-control
- Helps us to be observers of our thoughts, feelings, and emotions
- Allows us to be in the present moment
- Increases our ability to focus
- Helps us to be responsive rather than reactive
- Builds ability to tolerate stress
- Allows us to enjoy life more

We can be mindful, or pay attention on purpose, to anything we choose. One of the things it is helpful to pay attention to is our breath. By breathing in a certain way, we can actually change our mental and physiological state. This is because breathing is the only autonomic function we can control voluntarily. As such, it acts as a unique doorway into our autonomic nervous system. The breath creates a connection between our mind and our body and allows us to co-exist with physical and emotional discomfort. This book contains several focused breathing exercises for either calming down or ramping up our systems.

## Resilience

Resilience is the ability to adapt well mentally to stress, adversity, or tragedy without becoming overwhelmed. Resilience comes from a sense of agency—knowing that what we do makes a difference. From a physiological perspective, resilience means activating our stress response system when confronted with a threat and then returning to homeostasis, or a regulated state, when the threat has passed. Emotional and physical problems can happen when we remain in a heightened state.

There are ten tools that you can use to enhance your resilience:
1. Social connections
2. Self-esteem
3. Communication skills
4. Problem solving skills
5. Empowerment
6. Emotional and physical regulation
7. Flexible thinking
8. Setting and achieving goals
9. Self-care
10. Moral compass

## Yoga

What is yoga? What follows is a response from Yoga Alliance: "Answering the question, "What is Yoga?" is challenging and is the subject of extensive academic and philosophical study.

Yoga was developed up to 5,000 years ago in India as a comprehensive system for wellbeing on all levels: physical, mental, emotional and spiritual. While Yoga is often equated with Hatha Yoga, the well-known system of postures and breathing techniques, Hatha Yoga is only a part of the overall discipline of Yoga. Today, many millions of people use various aspects of Yoga to help raise their quality of life in such diverse areas as fitness, stress relief, wellness, vitality, mental clarity, healing, peace of mind and spiritual growth.

Yoga is a system, not of beliefs, but of techniques and guidance for enriched living. Among Yoga's many source texts, the two best known are the Yoga Sutras and the Bhagavad Gita. Both explain the nature of, and obstacles to, higher awareness and fulfillment, as well as a variety of methods for attaining those goals.

Since the individual experience of Yoga is quite personal and may differ for each practitioner, there are a wide variety of approaches to its practice. Yoga has in recent times branched out in many new directions, some of which are quite different from its traditional emphases. All approaches to Yoga, however, are intended to promote some aspect(s) of wellbeing."

The Yoga Sutras of Patanjali refer to eight limbs of yoga, only one of which is physical poses, or postures (Asana). Each limb offers guidance on how to live a meaningful and purposeful life:
1. Yama: Restraints, moral disciplines or moral vows
2. Niyama: Positive duties or observances
3. Asana: Posture
4. Pranayama: Breathing techniques
5. Pratyahara: Sense withdrawal
6. Dharana: Focused concentration
7. Dhyana: Meditative absorption
8. Samadhi: Bliss or enlightenment

Yoga means "union." One might say yoga is the union of the heart, mind, and body. Yoga helps us bridge the gap between *learning* about mental toughness skills and *being* mentally tough. This book includes a few simple postures for you to try. As you practice yoga and gain strength, flexibility and control over the body, you will also gain strength, flexibility, and control, or mental toughness, of the mind.

Yoga also helps your mental game by improving the following helpful self-regulatory senses:
1. Proprioception: An awareness of where your body is in space.
2. Interoception: An awareness of what is going on inside your body.

Yoga does all sorts of fantastic things for us. Beyond the physical benefits of improved balance, strength, flexibility, and agility, practicing yoga can reduce fears, help us feel more emotionally centered, decrease injuries, and increase focus. Yoga brings everything together and helps you create space in your mind and body for what serves you. Yoga is the perfect pairing for roller derby. Below are a few general guidelines to keep in mind when practicing the yoga poses in this book:
1. Be aware of the breath.
2. Breathe in and out through the nose.
3. Slow and deepen the breath.
4. When you are supporting your weight with your hands, spread your fingers wide and press evenly through your fingertips and the four corners of your hand.
5. When you are standing on your feet, spread your toes and press evenly through the four corners of each foot.
6. When in poses where your knee is bent, be sure it is positioned right over your ankle.

## Zen Derby

The concept of Zen derby encapsulates the core message of Zen. Not only is there no time like the present, there is no time *but* the present. The enlightened life is "This, Now." Zen is a practice of studying mind and seeing into one's nature. Zen is not an intellectual pursuit, but an experiential pursuit. It is a way of life. Zen is a school of Buddhism that emerged in China about 15 centuries ago, having strong roots in Taoism. It began to emerge as a distinct branch when the Indian sage, Bodhidharma taught at the Shaolin Monastery in China. Zen is the Japanese rendering of Ch'an which is the Chinese rendering of the Sanskrit word, Dhyana (the name for the 7th limb of yoga). Zen is known in Korea as Son and in Vietnam as Thien. In any language, it refers to a mind absorbed in meditation. The three aspects of Zen meditation, posture, breathing, and "no mind" meditation, calm the mind and form the path toward enlightenment—a state of mental clarity.

Even if you don't reach enlightenment, meditation has many benefits including improved concentration and self-understanding. We can live a more peaceful, less drama-filled life, when we acknowledge the space between events and our reaction to them. A 2011 study showed meditation to be such a powerful tool that it even changes brain structure! Practicing meditation increases grey matter in the Prefrontal Cortex through the process of neuroplasticity.

Elements of Zen that can be helpful to building your mental toughness are described in the guidelines of the Eightfold Path:

1. Right View. Being aware of your actions and the reasons behind them.

2. Right Intention. Having control over your actions. Not reacting to emotions such as jealousy or anger.
3. Right Speech. Being careful in the things you say. Speak friendly and only if you have something positive to say. Avoid hurtful words and lies.
4. Right Action. Don't do things that harm others such as bullying or stealing.
5. Right Livelihood. Living in an honest way.
6. Right Effort. Not causing harm, putting your efforts into what needs to be accomplished.
7. Right Mindfulness. The ability to observe your body, feelings, and mind. Being present, focused, and alert.
8. Right Concentration. Working to achieve one-pointedness of mind.

People with no religion or who practice other religions can and do practice Zen. It is very inclusive. It is a way of refining your life by carefully and directly observing your own mind. Zen emphasizes the responsibility of each of us for our own lives and the importance of one's own experience.

> *All that we are is the result of what*
> *we have thought.*
> *The mind is everything.*
> *What we think, we become.*
> *-Buddha*

# MENTAL TOUGHNESS TIP #1
## Celebrate Nice Falls

Don't freak out when you take a spill. This gives you and others the message that falling is bad. When you fall think, *That was awesome! Great fall, I'm so tough. That may bruise, but that's a mark of distinction.*

If it is a bigger fall that takes a moment to recover from, you can think, *That was a rough tumble. What did I do?* Figure out how to do it better the next time. Each fall is a learning experience.

*It's not how many times you fall that defines you, it's how many times you get up.*

# MENTAL TOUGHNESS TIP #2
## Get The Right Ingredients For Success

There are three ingredients for success and only one of them is completely under your control:

1. Luck. This includes things like "being at the right time and in the right place" and "who you know." Luck is awesome when it happens, but too much of it might make you doubt your abilities or decrease a sense of control over your own destiny.

2. Talent. This is your natural-born ability. The book, *The Sports Gene,* posits there are genetic gifts that cause some people to respond differently to training. Some people are also biologically more fearless or have other traits conducive to competitive sports. However, talent can be over-rated. 75% of talented teen athletes drop out of sports because they lose the fun and lack the mental toughness to compete at higher levels.

3. Hard Work. This is the ingredient you have control over so pile it on! Hard work can help make up for a lack of natural-born talent or happenstance. Answering the question of whether athletes are born or made, Joe Baker, a professor of kinesiology at Toronto's York University says putting in the work is essential to success— "Practice is the number one predictor of how good somebody gets at anything."

*Luck + Talent + Hard Work = Success*

# MENTAL TOUGHNESS TIP #3
## Stretch Out Of Your Comfort Zone

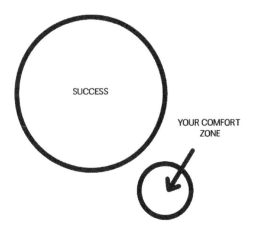

To get somewhere you've never been, you must do something you never have. We are all creatures of habit. The things that are the easiest for us to do are the ones we've always done. Staying in your comfort zone leads to plateauing and stagnation.

The concept, *neuroplasticity,* shows the brain can continuously change throughout our lifetime. It is flexible, like plastic. The pathways that are the strongest are the ones associated with the things we think, feel, and do the most often. These are our habits. When we think, feel, or do something new, it begins to rewire our brain. And the more you do this new thing, the stronger the new brain pathways will become.

Trying something new is most difficult the first time because those brain pathways are still weak. Sticking with new behaviors, cognitions, or emotional responses will cause them to become your new habits.

# MENTAL TOUGHNESS TOOL
## BE CALM: 4-7-8 BREATHING

Sit with your spine straight and legs uncrossed. Feel the support of the surface beneath you. Eyes can be open, closed, or your gaze softened. Bring your awareness to your breath and allow it to slow and deepen.

1. Close your mouth and inhale quietly through your nose to a mental count of four.
2. Hold your breath in the back of your throat for a count of seven.
3. Exhale slowly and completely through your mouth, making a whoosh sound to a count of eight. This is one breath cycle. Repeat three more times as follows:

    Breathe in    *1-2-3-4*
    Hold    1-2-3-4-5-6-7
    Breathe out    *1-2-3-4-5-6-7-8*

This exercise is a natural tranquilizer for the nervous system and a known remedy for panic attacks. Some people don't like practicing breath retention (holding the breath), so feel free to skip the hold part if it bothers you.

# MENTAL TOUGHNESS TIP #4
## Focus On Your Focus

To improve your performance, you need to understand how it is affected by your focus. Sports psychologist, Terry Orlick, suggests that when you understand what works well and what interferes, you can work on improving the consistency and quality of your focus.

1. Think of your best game.
2. What were you focused on before the game?
3. What did you focus on seconds before you started to play?
4. How would you describe your focused feeling during the game?
5. What were you focused on during the game?
6. Did you ever lose your focus?
7. If you did lose your focus, what did you do to get it back on track?
8. If you never lost focus, what kept you focused?

# MENTAL TOUGHNESS TIP #5
## Know The Benefits Of Stress

Learning that certain events or things in our environment lead to negative outcomes is essential to survival. When under stress or experiencing fear, our brain undergoes physical changes that make it better at processing information related to danger. Chemicals released into the brain during stress interact to trigger a "switch" that turns on a signal related to learning.

Under ordinary life circumstances, this may not serve us well. If a person is always stressed, they are going to be hypervigilant to signs that something bad is happening which will, of course, lead to more stress. In fact, individuals with clinical depression and anxiety are often unable to turn off this "switch" and constantly take in the negative messages around them. The debilitating emotional responses seen in Posttraumatic Stress Disorder are thought to involve this type of learning under stress.

But on the track, this is super helpful. The boost stress gives your ability to learn about and avoid the very real dangers around you helps you to survive and succeed.

# MENTAL TOUGHNESS TIP #6
## Tap Into Your Strengths

Look at this list of 24 character strengths. On the next page, write down your top five. They fall into the categories of strengths of wisdom, strengths of courage, strengths of humanity, strengths of temperance, and strengths of transcendence.

Creativity
Curiosity
Judgment
Perspective
Love of Learning
Bravery
Perseverance
Honesty
Zest
Love
Kindness
Social Intelligence
Teamwork

Fairness
Leadership
Forgiveness
Humility
Prudence
Self-Regulation
Appreciation of Beauty and Excellence
Gratitude
Hope
Humor
Spirituality

Once you have your top five strengths identified, narrow them down to your one biggest strength. Circle this strength. Think about ways you can use it to help you and/or your team in roller derby. By putting your strengths into action, it will solidify that you believe this to be true about yourself.

©Copyright 2004-2018, VIA Institute on Character. All Rights Reserved. Used with Permission. www.viacharacter.org

My top five strengths:

1.

2.

3.

4.

5.

This is how I will use my strength to help myself and/or my team:

_____

_____

# MENTAL TOUGHNESS TIP #7
**Pace Yourself**

When skaters know how to pace themselves, they will have a steady supply of high-level energy available to them for the entire game. Pacing involves knowing how much energy is required of you for a game, self-awareness about how much stored energy you have, and being able to dole out your energy in appropriate amounts. That way you don't run out before the game ends. Effective pacing also means not wasting energy on unnecessary things and being able to create more energy if you need it.

Using self-awareness and experience, a skater can learn their own signs of feeling sapped or whether they have a ton of energy left. Skaters can then adjust the way they are playing their game to be the best they can possibly be for the entire game. A skater can also learn how to store away the excess energy they have before a game for later. This is an excellent way to make use of the pre-game jitters.

### Storing Your Pre-game Energy For Later
1. Create a mental picture of the energy you have. What does your pre-game energy look like? Is it a small ball of fire? An animal? A lightning bolt?
2. Visualize yourself taking that energy and placing it somewhere inside of you where you will be able to draw on it when you need it.
3. Later in the game when you need some energy, tap the source. Picture yourself drawing on your inner energy source and allowing it to flood your entire body and mind.
4. Now you feel energized!

One source of energy drain is muscle use. A skater may use more muscle tension than necessary for a situation such as warming up. Another source of energy drain is anger, frustration, or fear. These emotions interfere with your best performance by wasting mental and physical energy that should be directed into your game. Skaters can learn how to transfer the energy that comes with these strong emotions into useful energy. One way to do this is by creating a mantra. A skater who feels angry can tell themselves they are going to transform their:

*Anger into strength,*
*Anger into speed, or*
*Anger into agility*

Repeating phrases like these manifest your thoughts into reality.

Another way to gain energy is to take it from your environment for your own use. Here are some potential places you can find energy:

1. The opposing team. If they are fired up, it can get you fired up too.
2. Your coach. Hearing an inspiring speech by your coach can be just what you need to find a little more energy.
3. Your teammates. When you see your teammates giving it everything they've got it will give you the strength you need.
4. The crowd. Get the audience cheering and it will help you to dig deep.

# MENTAL TOUGHNESS TOOL FOR TEAMS
## BE CONNECTED: FEEL THE PULSE

For this activity, have your team sit or stand in a circle, on-skates or off. Everyone will hold hands. One skater will start by squeezing the hand of the person to their right. When the person receiving the "pulse" feels it, they will then squeeze the hand of the skater to their right. The pulse will travel like this all the way around the circle and back to the first person.

Discuss what a pulse is (a short burst of energy or a measure of heartrate) and how it is vital for your team to be connected in heart, mind, and body. Try this before a game!

# MENTAL TOUGHNESS TIP #8
## Maximize Your Commitment

The words we use when talking about our goals can give us clues as to how ready we are to commit to them. There are four types of "change talk" we use when talking about our goals: resistance talk, stuck talk, change talk, and commitment talk. When we are resistant to working toward our goals, we may make excuses or blame circumstances or others outside of ourselves. Below are examples of resistance talk:
*The coach hates me*
*My gear sucks*
*They won't let me have a chance*

When we are stuck and not moving toward our goals, we may use words that show how dedicated to staying the same we are:
*I just don't get along with other females*
*I'm as fast as I can be*
*I will never hit as hard as him*

When we are starting to move toward making a commitment to achieving our goals we use change talk. Change talk includes the word "I" because it indicates we are starting to look inward at what we can do rather than outward at all the reasons we can't do it. Your change talk communicates a desire to achieve your goals, recognizes your ability to achieve your goals, and acknowledges a reason to achieve your goals. As you move from being motivated to achieve your goals to being committed to achieving your goals, your words will start to reflect that you are acting rather than just thinking about it.

Using words like these show a lower level of commitment:
 I hope to...
 I plan to...
 I will try to...

Words like these show a higher level of commitment:
 I will...
 I am going to...
 I promise to...

If you are not sure about committing to your goals, asking yourself questions like the following can help:
1. Suppose you don't work toward _____ (your goal), what do you think your life will be like one year from now?
2. If you were completely successful in achieving _____ (your goal), how would things be different for you?
3. On a scale from 1 to 10, how important is it for you to _____ (your goal)? What would need to happen to make that number go up?

When you have committed to your goals, your talk will be action-oriented and in the present tense because you will be doing it! Whatever you feed is going to grow. If you put your energy into talking about how you can't do something or don't want to do something, then not changing is going to gain power. If you talk about what you can do or are willing to do, or even better yet, *are* doing, those words will move you in the direction you want to go.

*Words are powerful.*

# MENTAL TOUGHNESS TIP #9
## Be Value-Driven

When we live a value-driven life, we make choices according to what really matters to us. It is a way to live without regrets.

If we are not acting in a value-driven way, we are acting in a way that is emotion-driven. To be emotion-driven means we make choices and decisions based on how we are *feeling* at any given time. The peril in this is the fleeting, uncontrollable nature of emotions. Emotions don't last, and they come and go without our having to do anything. If we respond according to how we are feeling, our actions are going to be inconsistent.

*I only did that because I was really angry.*
*I didn't try it because I felt scared.*
*I wasn't in the mood to do that drill.*

Our values, on the other hand, are fairly stable. Since consistency is the key to achieving your derby goals, values are a much better guide for your actions than emotions. Acting in a value-driven way will increase the likelihood that you will be successful on and off the track.

A full range of emotions enables us to fully experience all that life has to offer. However, some emotions can be difficult to endure (fear, worry, sadness, embarrassment, frustration, anger) so we try to avoid feeling them. When we are emotion-driven, our actions are geared toward feeling the "good" emotions (joy, pride, love, happiness, excitement, etc.) and avoiding the "bad" ones. But uncomfortable or even painful emotions such as disappointment, defeat, frustration, and anxiety are part of competitive sports. To try to avoid them is futile and diverts your energy from doing what you need to do to achieve your goals. This is how emotions can become barriers to achieving your potential.

Can you think of some emotions that get in the way of your success? In which situations do you feel these emotions? What actions typically follow these emotions? Realizing emotions are not the problem is key. It is the way we respond to them that is the problem.

Your values tell you why your goals are important to you. Your value-driven actions are the steady path you need to take to achieve your goals. By living according to your values, or what is most important to you, your practice and play will be more consistent.

To test whether you are acting in an emotion-driven or value-driven way, ask yourself, *Would I be acting like this if I was in a different mood?*

*(See page 218 to determine what your values are.)*

# MENTAL TOUGHNESS TOOL
## BE IN CONTROL: WOODCHOPPER

This exercise allows you to safely release stress, anger, frustration or other strong emotion. Begin with your legs wide apart and slightly bent. Clasp your hands over your head as if you are holding an axe. Imagine whatever emotion or situation you are dealing with is a piece of wood on the ground before you. Bring your hands down with a strong "chopping" motion while exhaling with a loud WHOOSH sound. Repeat several times.

# MENTAL TOUGHNESS TIP #10
## Take Calculated Risks

A brand-new skater might not want to try a 180 degree jump on their first day and a veteran skater shouldn't automatically say "No" to new challenges.

Learn how to assess risks to feel confident in your ability to take on challenges. Ask yourself what you know about the situation. What are the facts? Ask yourself what experiences or skills you have that will help you meet this challenge. Have you been able to do something similar in the past? Completing this type of risk assessment process enables you to look at a situation and say "Yes I can do this" or "No, this one's not safe. I'm going to make a smarter choice."

Don't automatically pass up challenges or this will become a pattern that is difficult to escape from and can lead to plateauing. At the same time, don't feel pressured to do things that you know are well beyond your abilities. By accurately assessing risks and taking on those challenges you feel are within your reach, your skills will continue to grow safely.

# MENTAL TOUGHNESS TIP #11
**Practice And Play With Intention**

Intentions are emotional qualities or attitudes we want to cultivate. They have physical, emotional, and spiritual aspects, allowing us to unify these domains. When you set an intention for a practice or game, you can focus on bringing this emotional quality or attitude into all that you do. Below are some popular intentions. Try setting an intention for your next practice or game by using this list or coming up with one of your own.

| | |
|---|---|
| Acceptance | Authenticity |
| Strength | Compassion |
| Kindness | Courage |
| Balance | Trust |
| Peace | Grace |
| Gratitude | Patience |

My Intention: _____

# MENTAL TOUGHNESS TIP #12
## Create Space

When we can separate ourselves from the internal processes of our thoughts and feelings, we become empowered because we realize we don't have to act on them. This means when you are angry, scared, frustrated, or other upsetting emotion, you don't have to let it get in the way of what you really want to be doing—being the best roller derby player you can be. Can you think of some situations in your life when you were able to create distance between what your mind told you and the believability of those thoughts?

Often, when we feel upset there is some event that happens outside of us. Perhaps a game situation makes us feel frustrated, angry, or worried. According to Stimulus-Response Theory, this event is the *stimulus*. After the stimulus occurs, we may respond with some unhelpful emotional response such as yelling, crying, throwing something, etc.

Stimulus ⟶ Response

Through the process of mindfulness, you can create a separation between yourself and your emotional responses. Imagine an upsetting roller derby situation in which you responded in an unhelpful way. Now imagine a different ending, one in which you acted in a way you are proud of. The space you create when choosing your responses is the "golden pause" and it makes all the difference.

Stimulus ⟶ SPACE ⟶ Response

*"Between stimulus and response there is a space. In that space is our power to choose our response. In that response lies our growth and our freedom."*

*-Viktor Frankl*

# MENTAL TOUGHNESS TIP #13
**Don't Choke**

Choking is when an athlete is unable to perform at their full potential in a high-pressure situation. This is something that can happen to jammers when games are on the line. Choking happens when an athlete becomes hyperconscious of skills they normally perform automatically. The thinking part of the brain is usually bypassed when performing skills that have been done a million times. During high-pressure situations, a skater may begin to overthink things and experience "paralysis by analysis," or choking.

The cure for choking is simple. Focus intently on something ordinary while waiting for the jam start whistle or while skating around the track in between scoring passes. You may have seen tennis players adjusting the strings on their racket prior to a serve or a basketball player bouncing the ball three times before a free throw. These simple routines occupy the thinking part of an athlete's brain and prevents it from trying to take over what should be fluid and automatic.

### First Aid For Choking

Here is an easy and effective way to get out of your head by focusing on your skates. Use this whenever you are having performance-interfering thoughts.

1. Bring your attention to your breath. Take a slow, deep breath in and out. As you exhale, allow your attention to drop down through your body, like a spider on a web, to your feet inside of your skates.
2. Notice how the bottoms of your feet feel with the support of your skates.

3. Notice how your skates feel against the skating surface that is supporting you.
4. If you are stationary awaiting the jam whistle, you can alternate between feeling "light" and "heavy" in your skates. If you are lapping to catch the pack, you can take a couple of mindful pushes.

   Your skates can act as an anchor for your attention, keeping your busy mind from those thoughts that can get in the way of your best performance.

# MENTAL TOUGHNESS TIP #14
**Form New Habits**

Adopt new habits that will facilitate your success. Elite athletes have developed daily habits including eating well, getting adequate sleep, workouts, and training.

There is a myth that new behavior will become a habit if a person does it for 21 days in a row. This is based on a misinterpretation of Dr. Maxwell Maltz' original work. What Maltz actually said was "it requires a minimum of about 21 days for an old mental image to dissolve and a new one to jell." Note the word *minimum*. 21 is not, as commonly believed, a magic number of days that solidifies a new behavior.

How long *will* it take for your new behavior to become a habit, or a part of your daily life? Recent research by Phillippa Lally, published in the *European Journal of Social Psychology,* found it takes an average of 66 days for a new behavior to feel automatic. It varied from 18 to 254 days! There are way too many individual elements to factor in to arrive at a one-size-fits-all amount of time. Getting focused on a number will only lead to frustration and feelings of defeat. Setting realistic expectations will help you to stay focused and not give up. Forming a new habit may take a long time and it will probably be a lot of work. But it will pay off in positive results.

How does one go about forming the daily habits of a successful athlete? Business coach, Tom Bartow, shares three steps to successful habit formation.

## Phase 1: The Honeymoon

This is when you feel like the task is easy. You may have had sudden inspiration to make a change.

## Phase 2: The Fight Through

This is when inspiration fades and reality begins to set in. You may find yourself struggling to stick to your new habit and want to return to old ones. To get to stage three and successfully form a new habit, you must win two or three "fight throughs." This is how you win a fight through:

a) Recognize: See what is happening for what it is. Tell yourself, "I am in a fight through and I need to win two or three of these to move past this."

b) Ask 2 Questions: Those two questions are, *How will I feel if I do this?* and H*ow will I feel if I don't do this?* Allow yourself to really experience the emotional fallout from each choice.

c) Life Projection: If you need to, imagine how your life will be in five years if you do not make this change now. Again, immerse yourself fully in the emotion of the projection.

## Phase 3: Second Nature

This phase feels like you are finding your groove. When you are in this phase there are three interruptions that can send you back to a fight through:

a) The Discouragement Monster: This is when you let negative results discourage you into thinking, *This isn't working.*

b) Disruptions: This can happen if you have a significant change to your daily patterns such as going on a vacation, getting ill, or have a work schedule change.

c) Seduction of Success: This happens when you begin to think you don't have to put in the hard work to maintain your positive results.

You may need to encounter a fight through many times throughout your life. Maintaining good daily habits won't always be easy, and it will take sacrifices. But that's what separates the best from the rest.

*Where you are now
doesn't determine how far you'll go.*

# MENTAL TOUGHNESS TIP #15
## Get In The Green Zone

This tip is adapted from Leah Kuyper's book, *Zones of Regulation*. Most people perform at their best when they are in a calm, yet alert state, primed and ready for anything that comes their way. This is the "Green Zone."

If you are too stressed out or your energy level is too low, create a plan to get where you need to be to perform at your best:
1. Assess which zone you are in.
2. Use the tools below to get into your Green Zone. Two ideas are provided. Try to come up with one of your own for each color.
3. Take steps to get into the Green Zone while you are in yellow and still have some control. Don't wait until you get into the Red Zone!

**If you are in the Blue Zone, try these tools...**

a. Have a teammate jump over you while you are laying down (pick somebody who has a proven track record for doing this safely).

b. Have an impromptu dance party.


c. _____

**If you are in the Yellow Zone, try these tools...**

a. Use 4-7-8 Breathing (see page 21).

b. Flip any unhelpful or irrational thoughts to helpful or rational ones (see page 98).


c. _____

**If you are in the Red Zone, try these tools...**

a. Sit with your back against the wall and place a jacket over your head (this satisfies the flight stress response).

b. Go for a fast, hard skate or run (this satisfies the fight response).

c. _____

Learn to assess and self-regulate your state so you can maximize your time in the Green Zone and optimize your performance.

**To stay in the Green Zone, try these tools...**

a. Get adequate sleep.

b. Spend quality time with those you care about.

c. _____

*Green means go!*

# MENTAL TOUGHNESS TIP #16
## Win Ugly

There is a concept in sports psychology called "winning ugly." This means getting the job done no matter how it looks. Practice is the time to hone your abilities, perfecting your technical, tactical, and mental skill sets. Games are for showing what you know.

You don't need perfect form, technique, or strategy to pull off a win. Winning ugly is evidence that perfection is unnecessary to win. You can still succeed when you are not on top of your game. Some athletes tend to back down when they are not playing well in a game. These athletes send negative messages to themselves like:

*We're so far down, why even try.*
*There is no way we can come back from this.*
*We're not going to win with how terrible I'm skating.*

Winning ugly can be a valuable concept to keep athletes motivated when a game isn't going their way or they feel like they are having an off day. They can grit their teeth, push forward, and be resilient regardless of the circumstances. The mentally tough athlete needs perseverance, a positive attitude, and a present-moment focus. Keep fighting until the end because it is that fight that keeps your chances for a victory alive.

# MENTAL TOUGHNESS TOOL
## BE SHINING: STAR POSE

Stars have been a source of mystery and wonder ever since people first looked up to them. They provide direction and inspiration. Stars are strong, creating their own gravitational force. Our own sun is a star and gives us warmth and light.

This pose develops a sense of center, balance, and personal power. From standing, take your feet wide and point your toes straight ahead. Take your arms out to the sides and parallel to the earth. Engage your muscles and extend out through arms, legs, and head. Spread your fingers like the rays of the sun. Hold for three to five breaths.

While in this pose, you can ask yourself the following questions:
1. What guides me?
2. How do I shine like a star?
3. Can I shine on my own and be part of a galaxy?

# MENTAL TOUGHNESS TIP FOR TEAMS #17
## Keep Your Head In The Game When Your Team is Down

You're in the last 15 minutes of the game and your team is down in points. How do they react? Does your team give up? Do you decide that you've already lost when the game isn't over? Are you imagining how refreshing that cool beverage will be at the afterparty? If so, those thoughts can impact the final score. Your thoughts can transform into reality. When your team is down, you must decide whether to play harder or give up. Here are some ways to help you and your team keep their head in the game and make a decision to play harder!

**Get your game face on.** A skater's non-verbal communication, body language, and facial expressions, make up 60-70% of their message. Look aggressive and ready. If your body and face is in battle-mode, your brain will get the message. This will also help your teammates because they will be less likely to give up if they see you are still in the fight.

**Cheer.** Create a team cheer or chant that motivates everyone to keep fighting until the bitter end. If you're going out, go out in a blaze of glory!

"Get out of our way, we're gonna blow you away!"

**Think positively.** A lot can happen in a single jam. Being down by 15 points can turn into being up by 15 points in two jams. Think positive thoughts like, *We can win this,* and performance will improve.

**Turn to your spirit leaders.** There are skaters on every team that seem to have sunshine shooting out of their rear-ends. When the going gets tough, get those skaters to boost your team's morale. This can be a great role for a newer skater to take on. It can show that all members of the team are crucial, regardless of differences in skill level.

**Change strategies.** If your team is suffering a detrimental point spread that it is impossible to recover from, change the way you measure a win. For example, you could focus on staying out of the penalty box so a full lineup can go out every jam. Finding success with a goal that you control may even bring the inner-strength and confidence needed to pull off a miracle win.

**Think of what's best for the team.** When a team is down in points, game strategy may have to change. Less seasoned skaters may find themselves sitting on the bench. Having a pity-party can negatively affect your teammates. You are a member of the team and the win (or loss) will belong to all, regardless of skate time.

# MENTAL TOUGHNESS TIP #18
## Stay Hydrated

Drinking water boosts your mental performance. A 2013 article in *Military Medicine* showed losing as little as 1% of one's body weight in fluids reduced brain function in pilots. Getting dehydrated can negatively influence memory, attention, energy, spatial orientation, and other aspects of cognitive performance. Getting dehydrated can also lead to feelings of anxiety and depression.

If losing 1% of your body's mass in water can happen during everyday life, imagine how much water you can lose during extreme sports such as roller derby. How much water do you need to drink? Many sources cite 64 ounces per day as a general recommendation.

Below are some guidelines for athletes. You will want to create a customized plan that meets the needs of your physiology and the demands of the activity (including intensity and temperature):

- Two hours before a game or practice, drink 16 ounces of water
- Drink 8 ounces of water for every sugary or caffeinated drink you consume before or during a game or practice
- 10 to 20 minutes before a game or practice, drink another 8 ounces
- Every 15 to 20 minutes during the activity, drink a full 8 ounces
- Following the competition or practice, drink 16 to 24 ounces for every pound of body weight lost.

Watery drinks including teas, low-fat milk, coffee, and sugar-free drinks also count. Be aware that caffeinated drinks can make you have to pee more often. You can also get water from the foods you eat such as soup, ice cream, fruits, and veggies. Water from foods can make up around 20% of our total water intake per day.

Feeling thirsty is a common early sign that you haven't been drinking enough water. Signs of dehydration include dark-colored urine, feeling lethargic, dizziness, or having a dry mouth and lips.

There is real danger for athletes in drinking *too much* water because they are sweating out water and electrolytes. Drinking too much water increases the amount of water in the blood. This extra water dilutes the electrolytes there, especially sodium. This can lead to a condition called water intoxication and hyponatremia (low sodium levels) which involves the swelling of brain cells.

Staying properly hydrated will lead to improved mood, more energy, better sleep cycles, feelings of calmness, and satisfaction. This also improves cognition including spatial orientation, memory, and focus. Hydration levels can have a major impact on your performance, mentally and physically. Bottoms up!

# MENTAL TOUGHNESS TOOL
## BE SELF-AWARE: MENTAL TOUGHNESS QUIZ

Return to take this quiz periodically to assess where you are in your mental toughness skills.

1. Before a game I...
a) Always set goals
b) Sometimes set goals
c) Never set goals

2. Whether I am winning or losing I...
a) Always believe in myself
b) Believe in myself only when I am winning
c) Rarely believe in myself and think I'm a failure

3. Distractions during a game...
a) Don't bother me
b) Sometimes bother me, but I can easily refocus
c) Take my focus fully away from my performance

4. My emotions, thoughts, and breathing during a game are usually...
a) Something I can control and use to my advantage
b) Inconsistent, but are in my control when I am doing well
c) Not in my control, my breathing is too fast, and I have a hard time reacting

5. After a game, the self-evaluation of my performance is...
a) Normally accurate about what my strengths and weaknesses were that day

b) Not always accurate, but I can pick out some key things I need to improve
c) Never accurate because I don't ever evaluate my performance

### Answers
a's are worth 3 points each
b's are worth 2 points each
c's are worth 0 points each

12-15: You are very mentally tough
8-11: You are somewhat mentally tough
4-7: You could benefit from more mental toughness
0-3: Uh oh, you need to learn some mental toughness skills

# MENTAL TOUGHNESS TIP #19
## Keep Your Power

To be mentally tough, you need all the mental strength you can get. This strength is experienced as a sense of competence, positive attitude, confidence, and vision—our personal power. But sometimes we unintentionally give our power away. Amy Morin, author of *13 Things Mentally Strong People Don't Do,* tells us giving away our power decreases our mental strength. Here are some things you can do to keep your power and control over your performance.

**Stop complaining.** Focusing on problems rather than solutions implies you have no power to change your situation. Instead of thinking, *I suck*, think, *What can I do to improve?*

**Practice forgiveness.** Are you still holding a grudge against a teammate, coach, or official? When you hold a grudge, it is *you* that carries the weight of the anger, frustration, or hate. To forgive someone doesn't mean you're forgiving behavior, it means you are choosing to let it go so those emotions aren't interfering with your ability to give your best performance.

**Identify your values.** Your journey to success needs a map and your values are the guide you need to stay on track. Identify what is important to you about roller derby. Think about yourself as an athlete and as a teammate. Constantly check to see if your actions honor your values.

**Accept responsibility for your emotions and actions.** When somebody *makes* you mad or frustrated or distracted you are essentially saying they control you. Don't give someone else the reins!

**Avoid victim language.** Let the words you use reflect the power you have. By using the statements below, it implies you have no choice or control:
"My coach made me jam."
"I had to skate 3 jams in a row."

*Choose strong language that shows your power:*
"I was brave and took the jammer pantie."
"It was tough, but I was able to skate 3 jams in a row."

**Create your own self-esteem.** If you only feel good about yourself when you get positive feedback from others, you are making yourself dependent on external circumstances to feel good. Receiving feedback from others can be inconsistent and outside of your control. Develop an internal reward system in which you are driven by the personal meaning you derive from this sport. Ask yourself, *Why do I do this?* Focus on those elements that are under your control.

# MENTAL TOUGHNESS TIP #20
## Set Short-term Goals

The first step in undertaking any journey is to decide where you want to go. Solid roller derby goals guide our actions and give us direction. Goals allow us to know when we are on track and when we have wandered. You should have a short-term, achievable goal in mind for every practice or game.

Your short-term goal does not have to be about skating. You can create goals around things like not arguing with the coach, remembering your water bottle, supporting teammates, or stretching after you skate.

Achieving your short-term goals will help you achieve your long term, loftier roller derby goals. Here are some examples of practice goals:

- I will pay attention when the coach is talking
- I will volunteer first
- I will talk to someone I don't know well
- I will try something new
- I will challenge myself by attacking the biggest threat rather than the weakest link
- I will leave my bad day at the door

My short-term goal for the next practice:

_____

_____

Here are some examples of game goals:
- I will get zero penalties
- I will be on time
- I will keep my cool if an opponent trash talks me
- I will watch for the coach telling me to call the jam
- I will high-five my teammates when they come off the track
- I will smile at the end of the game, win or lose

My short-term goal for the next game:

_____

_____

## MENTAL TOUGHNESS TOOL
### BE REMEMBERED: CREATE YOUR OWN LEGACY

Imagine it is 20 years from now and your friends and family are sitting around a table sharing stories about your roller derby career. How would you like your career and you as an athlete to be remembered? What kinds of things would you want to hear them say about you? This activity will help you identify those qualities, in heart, mind, and body, that you want to cultivate. Write your roller derby story in the space provided.

**My Story**

_____

_____

_____

_____

# MENTAL TOUGHNESS TIP FOR TEAMS #21
## Crush Cliques

Cliques are small groups who interact with one another more than other members of the team. These groups benefit those few involved and alienate the rest of the team. Cliques are usually formed when the team is losing, when coaches treat skaters differently, or when skaters' needs are not being met. A clique is different than a group of friends. Cliques are typically exclusive, restrictive, and focused on maintaining their status as being better than the rest of the team. Cliques can be extremely destructive to a team, especially when they are made up of skilled or popular skaters that others look up to. A clique can create a toxic league environment as more and more skaters emulate their negative behavior. Here are a few ideas for crushing cliques, turning that tightly closed cliquey circle into an open 'U':

1. Encourage an inclusive culture. Communicate regularly that your team's power is in its diversity. Create an understanding that all team members are equally welcome and valuable.
2. Make new groups. When practicing drills or scrimmaging, separate clique members into different groups to force them to interact with others.
3. Involve the "queen pins." Get your team's formal and informal leaders on board. See what ideas they may have for destroying the clique.
4. Use "atta-girls." When cliques do dissolve, use positive praise. Allow the clique members to know their positive behavior is noticed and appreciated.

# MENTAL TOUGHNESS TIP #22
## Achieve A State Of Coherence

There is a reciprocal relationship between our physiological, cognitive, and emotional systems. A principal pathway for our emotional wellbeing is the connection between our heart and our brain. In fact, our heart sends more information to our brain than our brain does to our heart. Heart rate variability (HRV) is the variation in time intervals between heart beats. HRV is controlled by our autonomic nervous system (ANS) which, using information gathered in the hypothalamus, sends signals to the rest of the body to either stimulate or relax certain functions.

In healthy individuals, the two branches of the ANS, the sympathetic nervous system and the parasympathetic nervous system, work together to keep us in balance. Every time you inhale, the sympathetic nervous system ramps your system up and every time you exhale, the parasympathetic nervous system calms everything down.

High HRV means there is a healthy irregularity in the time between heart beats, meaning our system is functioning well and is in a state of *coherence.* This is a term used by the Institute of HeartMath to describe a highly efficient psychological and physiological state in which your nervous system, cardiovascular, hormonal, and immune systems are working together efficiently and harmoniously.

HRV is a significant marker of health and fitness, resilience, and behavioral flexibility. An analogy for high HRV is a blocker who is shifting their weight between their two skates, staying light, loose, and prepared to spring into action, ready to adapt depending on where the opposing jammer heads. Low HRV would be a blocker with weight centered on both skates and muscles tensed, causing them to be slow to react to direction changes made by the opposing jammer.

If a person's HRV is low, it indicates they are living in flight or fight mode. The stress response system isn't returning to a resting state once the danger has passed. This indicates one's system is not as prepared to handle stress as it could be.

The pattern of your heart rhythm reflects your emotional state. Low HRV has been associated with depression and anxiety. When you are feeling irritable, impatient, frustrated, or anxious, your heart rhythm shifts into a disordered and incoherent pattern (see the top graph on the next page). Due to the reciprocal nature of the heart to brain pathway, we can change our emotional state by changing our heart rhythm.

How do you get into this state of coherence? The Institute of HeartMath developed a simple yet powerful technique called Quick Coherence that enables you to recharge in as little as three to five minutes. Using this technique a couple times a day brings you more inner clarity and balance (see bottom graph on the next page).

**Steps for Quick Coherence Technique**

Step 1: Begin to breathe in for five seconds and out for five seconds, counting silently as you breathe

Step 2: Make a sincere attempt to experience a regenerative feeling such as appreciation or care for someone or something in your life.

Suggestion: Try to re-experience the feeling you have for someone you love, a pet, a special place, an accomplishment, etc. or focus on a feeling of calm.

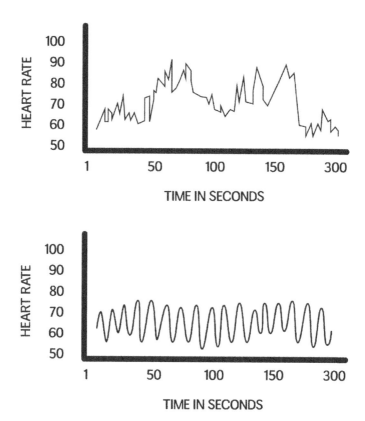

# MENTAL TOUGHNESS TOOL
## BE FOCUSED: EXPERIENCE YOUR FOCUSING AND DEFOCUSING NETWORKS

The practice of shifting our attention from one feeling to another, or from one thought to another, involves moving from the focusing to the defocusing networks of your brain. This process shifts you from being stuck in unhelpful feelings and actions and enables you to connect to an infinite world of possibilities. Your defocusing networks enable you to recognize actions that empower you in your life. You can unlearn old patterns of reactive behavior and rewire new strategies into your brain. The following guided meditation is adapted with permission from the book, *The iRest Program for Healing PTSD.*

With your eyes open, welcome the environment and sounds around you, the touch of air on your skin, the sensations where your body touches the surface that's supporting it.
Bring your attention to an object that's out in front of you. Direct your attention to this object alone. Exclude all other objects that are around you and focus only on this one object. Focus on the object's size, color, shape, and form. Note particular thoughts you have about it.
Now, take in all the objects around you without focusing on any particular object, color, shape, or form. Allow your attention to relax and defocus. Soften your eyes. Instead of looking with your eyes, sense from your heart as you take in all the objects around you, out in front, to your right and left, behind you. Sense all these directions at once. Feel like you're looking

everywhere, without focusing on anything specific. Now shift your attention back to the particular object you were first focusing on. Bring it into sharp focus. Then soften your eyes and feel yourself looking everywhere again. Defocus your attention. Don't focus on anything specific.

Go back and forth several times, focusing and defocusing your attention, and experience the effect this has on your body and mind.

Now try the same exercise with your eyes closed. Sense an internal object, a sensation, an emotion, or a thought. Focus your attention on this internal object alone. Then shift your attention so that you feel like you're looking everywhere, without focusing on anything specific. Then shift your attention back to a particular internal object, then feel yourself looking everywhere again. Go back and forth several times, focusing and defocusing your attention with your eyes closed, and experience the effect this has on your body and mind. When you're ready, allow your eyes to slowly open and close several times. Feel yourself present to this moment as you come fully back to your wide-awake state of mind and body.

# MENTAL TOUGHNESS TIP #23
## Have Just the Right Amount Of Confidence

Confidence can be defined in three ways: overconfidence, lack of confidence, and optimal confidence.

1. Overconfidence is when one's confidence is greater that their abilities. This is being falsely confident. It is not overconfidence if your confidence is based on your actual skills and abilities.
2. One's confidence is lacking if they have the physical skills to be successful but are not able to perform these skills. Self-doubt undermines your performance by creating anxiety, breaking your concentration, and causing indecisiveness.
3. Your confidence is at an optimal level when you are so convinced you can achieve your goals that you strive hard to do so. Optimal confidence is essential to reaching your potential.

The figure on the following page shows the relationship between performance and confidence. As your confidence goes up, so will your performance. However, if you become overconfident, your performance does not keep pace. You will perform the best under optimal confidence conditions.

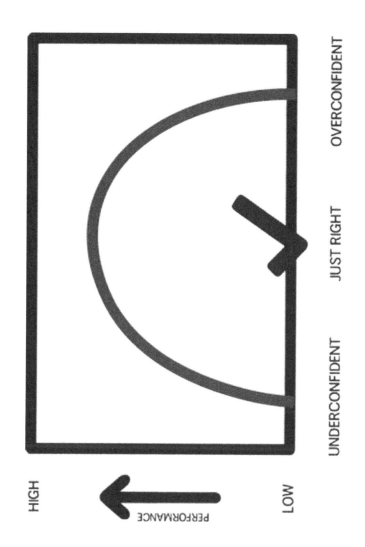

# MENTAL TOUGHNESS TIP #24
## Double Your Happiness

Shawn Anchor, positive psychologist and author of *The Happiness Advantage,* has come up with some ways to achieve long term happiness. One of these is called "The Doubler." This is a daily habit that involves telling another person about a positive experience you had. In the retelling, you will have effectively doubled your happiness.

You can double your happiness in this sport by telling someone about a positive roller derby experience you had. Here are some possibilities to give you inspiration:
- Witnessing a teammate doing something incredible
- Making progress learning a new skill
- Sharing about something funny happening at practice
- Successfully executing a strategic play
- Observing amazing sportsmanship
- Dealing with something tough in a way you are proud of

Share your positive roller derby experience with someone and double your happiness today!

# MENTAL TOUGHNESS TOOL
## BE MINDFUL: BREATH COUNTING

Try this deceptively simple Zen mindfulness practice. This exercise will help you learn self-awareness, be in the present moment, and create distance between your thoughts and feelings and your actions.

1. Sit in a comfortable position with the spine straight and head inclined slightly forward.
2. Gently close your eyes or soften your gaze and take a few slow, deep breaths. Then let the breath come naturally without trying to influence or change it in any way
3. To begin the exercise, count "one" to yourself as you exhale.
4. The next time you exhale, count "two" and so on up to "ten."
5. Then begin a new cycle, counting "one" on the next exhalation.
6. Never count higher than ten and count only when you exhale.

At some point, you may realize that you are thinking about something else besides breathing and counting. Or you may find yourself counting to "twelve" or even "twenty." If you notice that your mind has wandered, as minds tend to do, gently bring your attention back to the task at hand, starting again at "one." In that moment of realization, you have come back to the present moment. Try to do 5 minutes of this meditation to start. Set a timer so you don't need to worry about checking a clock.

# MENTAL TOUGHNESS TIP #25
**Don't Sweat The Small Stuff**

Keeping the peace on your team is more valuable than making a big fuss about something you will have forgotten about in a couple of days. Are you the type of skater who isn't bothered by anything? Are you the type that makes an issue out of every single thing that comes up? Can you find a balance between these two types of responses?

The strong emotional reaction of our downstairs brain is going to make us think situations are urgent and need to be dealt with RIGHT NOW. This is true for situations that make us feel betrayed, humiliated, or rejected. In other words, situations that make us feel emotional danger. As you start becoming mentally tough and develop self-control, you will be able to look back and say, "Wow I'm really proud of how I handled that situation."

Be slower to judge something that happens as being "good" or "bad." If enough time passes, we can often look back and see that things we thought were unlucky or bad at the time turned out to be fortunate.

To practice the skill of not sweating the small stuff, make a mental list of all the times that you have been upset in derby. Which of the buckets described on the next page would you put these issues into?

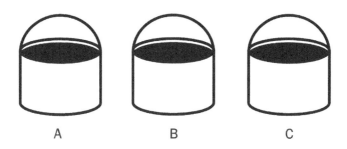

**Bucket A:** These are Big Problems. Bucket A problems are serious issues that absolutely need to be addressed immediately and include health and safety concerns such as bullying, racism, or sexual harassment.

**Bucket B:** These are Medium Problems. These are negotiable, meaning you try to work these problems out with the others involved. It is not imperative that you get your way 100% and compromise may be the solution. Small issues that are continuing to bother you also go into this category. By dealing with these Bucket B problems you are preventing them from turning into larger ones. Examples are: being bothered by cliques at practice, coach "favorites," or the way a teammate communicates with you.

**Bucket C:** These are Small Problems. They are things that you can let go without bringing them up. After a short period of time these problems no longer bother you. You can usually solve small problems on your own. Minor annoyances fall into this category such as when a teammate drinks out of your water bottle without asking.

# MENTAL TOUGHNESS TIP #26
**Ride The Fear**

Imagine you're standing at the top of a zip line landing looking down a speedy, 200-foot ride through the forest canopy and you're afraid of heights. Your heart is beating fast, your muscles are tensing up, and your breathing is rapid. All the signals from your body are telling you there is danger here. These are your smoke alarms going off. Then you jump off and have an exhilarating ride. This is a healthy response to feelings of fear. One should acknowledge the alarms, assess the situation, and then decide to go for it or not. Fear alone should not make the decision for you. You can decide to ride (or override) the fear.

Learn to recognize the sensations of fear in your body for what they are—an alarm system. It takes your thinking brain, or your "watchtower," to determine whether there is a fire.

In the zip line example above, the feelings of fear are in response to sensory input about how high up you are. If we become solely focused on this then we may not be able to jump off. We may become paralyzed by fear and respond as if it is a life-threatening situation. To jump, we must take into consideration all the signs of safety such as the protective harnesses, the training we are given, our past experiences, our helpful guide, and the fact that thousands of people have done it before us without incident. Then we can go for it. And the more times you do it, the easier it becomes. It may even eventually become fun!

Fear loses its grip on you when you learn to recognize the fear response and realize you can choose to override it.

*"You can't stop the waves,
but you can learn to surf."*

*-Jon Kabat-Zinn*

# MENTAL TOUGHNESS TIP #27
## Challenge Self-Doubts

Take a moment to imagine what living your full potential would look and feel like. Achieving your full potential means doing everything you can, despite irrational fears, self-doubts, and worries.

Self-doubt means we question ourselves and our ability to be successful. Sometimes it may be difficult to battle self-doubts because we really believe they are accurate and not just something our mind is telling us. Follow the steps below to challenge any self-doubts that hold you back.

1. Think of some self-doubts that interfere with your performance.
2. When do these self-doubts come up? Are there certain situations or circumstances that trigger them?
3. Determine the origins of these self-doubts. Whose voice is it?
4. What is the evidence that these self-doubts are true?
5. Look for evidence that they aren't true. This step begins to create flexibility in your thinking.
6. The opposite of doubt is confidence and trust. One must have confidence and trust in their abilities to succeed. What do you want to believe about yourself?
7. Continually seek evidence that this opposite is true. If you doubt your abilities, replace that thought with what you want to believe.

# MENTAL TOUGHNESS TIP #28
## Give Great Feedback

1. Give specific feedback. Don't tell a skater instruction such as "Focus!" This doesn't provide any technical information needed for skaters to correct their mistakes. Instead of "Focus!" say "Look for their jammer."

2. Cushion the correction between positive messaging. One method for correcting errors is the Hamburger Method. State the correction, or the "meat" of the message, between two positive messages making it easier to take.

3. Demand effort, not results. Skaters should be praised for correct techniques regardless of the outcome. If they do everything right except make the block they should get positive reinforcement saying, "Good effort" or "Good idea!"

4. Don't give too many corrections at once. Pick one thing for the skater to focus on, not a whole list of things. If you say, "Stay low, get your swivel head on, stay with your blockers, keep your eye on the jammer and watch out for that sweep!" the skater is going to be overwhelmed and probably not focus on any of those items. Overcorrecting leads to feelings of defeat and incompetence.

5. Focus on what you want skaters to do, not what you don't want them to do. Instead of "Don't go out of bounds," "Don't look down," or "Don't get any penalties," state the action you want them *to* take such as, "Stay in bounds," "Keep your eyes forward," or "Skate careful and clean."

6. Keep praise focused on their abilities. Don't ever tell skaters they accomplished something due to luck or because the task was an easy one.

7. Always give genuine, sincere feedback. Avoid saying "Good job" or "That was great!" if the skater knows it wasn't.

8. Use minimal words. Avoid lengthy explanations or directions. 25 words is the maximum amount you should use. Preferably keep feedback short, sweet, and to the point.

9. Think before you speak. Follow the old saying, "If you can't say something nice, don't say anything at all." Is what you want to say necessary? Is it inspiring? Is it helpful? Words can be incredibly powerful, and you don't want to cause more harm than good.

10. Tell, Show, Do. Briefly explain what to adjust. Perhaps give a short demonstration. Then have them try it out. Repeat these steps as necessary.

# MENTAL TOUGHNESS TIP #29
**Put On The Pressure**

We often think of stress or pressure as a bad thing. But we need a certain amount of it to be motivated. If we are too relaxed, we won't have the energy to do our best. As the figure on the following page shows, our performance improves as the amount of pressure increases. However, this is only true up to a certain point and then our performance starts to fall off. Too much pressure will negatively affect our performance, making us overwhelmed and unable to function.

Get to know yourself and what works best for you. Then try to make it a consistent part of your routine. How much stress or pressure do you need to perform at your best? Ask yourself the following questions to understand the connection between your stress levels and your performance.

1. Think about your best game or practice. Where was your stress level?
2. If needed, what did you do to energize?
3. If needed, what did you do to relax?
4. Give your ideal stress level a name (some ideas are below).

I perform best when I am:

_____

(Cool, Chill, Calm, Energized, Wild, Hyper, Crazy)

Find your ideal stress level on this graph and mark it with an 'X.' This is your pressure target zone.

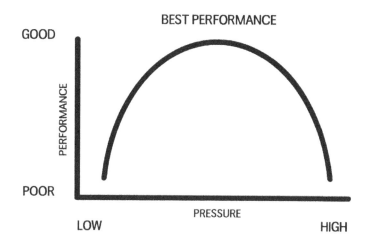

# MENTAL TOUGHNESS TOOL
## BE CONNECTED: TRIANGLE POSE

A triangle is very strong, which is why you see its shape used in the building of bridges and other structures. A triangle has three sides which are the minimum needed to make a shape or fully support something (think of a 3-legged chair, camera tripod, or tricycle).

Stand with your legs wide apart. Turn your right foot to face forward. Your right heel will be aiming toward the arch of your left foot. Lift your arms up parallel to the earth. Inhale and as you exhale, reach your right arm and torso forward and stretch your right hand down to your shin or surface outside your right foot, depending on how flexible you are. Keep both of your legs straight. Stretch your left arm up toward the sky, activating your muscles from your feet all the way up to your left finger tips. Look up toward your left hand if that feels comfortable. Repeat on the other side.

As you work with this pose, be aware of what is happening within your mind and body. As you hold this pose, it may be enlightening to think about the following:
1. What are three of my strengths?
2. When do I become unstable?
3. How do my thoughts, feelings, and actions interact?

## MENTAL TOUGHNESS TOOL
### BE ENERGIZED: OUTER QI SHOWER

This Qi Gong technique enlivens and brings energy to the mind and body. Gently slap the areas as described below.

1. Slap the belly with an alternating rhythm.
2. Slap the chest with an alternating rhythm.
3. Slap with one hand under one arm down the side of the ribs and then do the other side.
4. Slap down the inside of one arm to the palm, then up the outside of the hand and arm to the shoulder. Repeat on your other arm.
5. Use an alternating rhythm to slap up the face and sides of the head to the top of the skull, down the back of the cranium, and down the neck.
6. Slap the kidneys and low back with both hands (alternating side to side each slap) and down to the sacrum.
7. Slap the hands down the outside of the legs in a simultaneous rhythm. Repeat on back, front, and insides of legs.

# MENTAL TOUGHNESS TIP #30
## Be The Lion, Not The Dog

Automatic behaviors are the things we do without making a conscious decision to do them. This happens because we have developed patterns in how we react to certain thoughts, feelings, and situations. Automatic behaviors are problematic when they aren't helping us achieve our goals. Many times, we develop these kinds of patterns in response to negative or upsetting emotions. The emotions don't feel good, so we react in an attempt to avoid them. These tactics can help relieve discomfort in the short run, but they don't help you achieve your goals. The opposite of automatic behaviors are mindful behaviors. These are the behaviors we consciously and purposefully choose to make. We are in control of our mindful behaviors.

Honest self-awareness is necessary as you begin to unlearn automatic behaviors that don't work and replace them with new, helpful behaviors. Self-awareness will also help you understand that emotions are experiences that don't need to be controlled or avoided, even negative ones common in competitive sports such as fear, embarrassment, or disappointment.

Sam Himelstein, founder of the Center for Adolescent Studies, came up with a great analogy that demonstrates the striking difference between automatic behaviors and mindful behaviors. Think of how a dog acts when a person is waving a bone in front of its face. The dog will be consumed by that bone, turning its head every which way to follow the bone. Now what will happen if the person throws the bone? The dog will go after it. Consider the same scenario with a lion. What will the lion do if a person waves a bone in front of its face and then throws it? Is the lion going to chase the bone? It could chase the bone. Or it could eat the person.

When the bone is being waved in front of its face, the dog sees nothing but the bone. The bone represents all of the dog's reality, consuming the dog. The lion's mind, on the other hand, is a lot different. The lion can see past one aspect of the situation to the bigger picture and can make the most sensible decision. The lion thinks, *Doesn't this person know they have way more bones in their body?* The bone is just a sliver of the lion's larger reality. This gives the lion the ability to choose and have more control over itself.

Our emotions can rule us in the same way the bone controls the dog. Emotions can overtake us and become our whole reality. With mindfulness practice you can experience your emotions as just one aspect of a much bigger picture, one in which you don't let emotions get in the way of achieving your dreams. The process of being mindful will create space between you and your emotions and allow you to respond in the way you want instead of reacting automatically.

*Remember the lion-mind.*
*Be the king of your inner jungle.*

# MENTAL TOUGHNESS TOOL FOR TEAMS
## BE TRUSTING: RELATIONSHIP EXERCISES

Here are three relationship building exercises that will help your team build trust with one another.

1. Look into one another's eyes for 60 seconds. Partner up and gaze at each other. It is okay to laugh.
2. Give each other compliments. Switch partners in between each exercise. With your new partner, take turns giving one another genuine compliments.
3. Ask three questions. Switch partners again and take turns asking the other person three questions. Here are some ideas below:
   a) Why did you choose your jersey number?
   b) Fill in the blank: If you really knew me, you'd know _____.
   c) What superpower would you like to have?
   d) If you could be any animal, what would you be?
   e) What is your favorite song?
   f) How do you recharge?
   g) What characteristic do you admire most in others?
   h) What's the craziest thing you've ever done?
   i) What's your pet peeve?
   j) What's your secret talent no one knows about.
   k) If you could go anywhere in the world, where would it be?
   l) What would you bring to a potluck?
   m) Do you have any phobias?
   n) Do you collect anything?
   o) What's the best advice you ever heard?

# MENTAL TOUGHNESS TIP #31
## Know The Difference Between Discomfort And Pain

There is a difference between physical discomfort and pain, and emotional discomfort and pain. Physical discomfort means your body is getting stronger. Physical pain means a potential injury. Emotional discomfort means you are outside of your comfort zone. This may lead to uncomfortable emotions such as sadness, loneliness, disappointment, anxiety, fear, or agitation. Emotional pain means your heart and mind are being injured. Emotional pain occurs when one experiences things like harassment, bullying, loss, or terror. Pain is a warning sign that what is happening is overwhelming your resources. Pain tells you when something is wrong. Becoming mentally tough means being able to deal with some discomfort, but not pain.

# MENTAL TOUGHNESS TIP #32
## Have A Positive Attitude

Attitude counts! Having a great attitude is just as essential as having great skating skills. What exactly does it mean to have a great attitude? Here it is broken down into some actions you can take:

- Taking feedback without arguing or getting defensive
- Being inspired by the awesome skaters on your team rather than feeling jealous or threatened
- Giving instructions to teammates without anger or frustration
- Supporting your team at games even when you didn't get rostered
- Doing what needs to be done for the greater good of the team
- Helping up and coming skaters
- Not making excuses or blaming others, being accountable for your own actions
- Staying optimistic when your team is down in points

When you have a positive attitude you feel good and your teammates also feel good. This is due to our brain's mirror neurons or "empathy neurons." These neurons respond in the same way when we experience an emotion and when we observe someone else experiencing that same emotion. As neuroscientist V.S. Ramachandran says, the only thing separating one person from another is our skin. We are all truly connected.

If you're looking for an easy way to spread positivity to yourself and others, you just need to smile!

This can improve your mood and reduce stress, even if it is a fake smile. Just make sure it is a big one. Smile all the way up to the muscles around the eyes to get the effects.

# MENTAL TOUGHNESS TOOL
## BE FOCUSED: FOCUS TRAINING EXERCISE I

To play at their best, an athlete must direct their attention from distracting or unhelpful internal experiences to relevant external elements. In this exercise, you will work on shifting your focus from upsetting thoughts and uncomfortable feelings such as those below to the necessary elements of the task at hand. For these exercises you will think of three upsetting roller derby situations you have experienced—one difficult, one challenging, and one threatening. Then follow the directions to train your focus.

**Upsetting thoughts:**
*How am I doing?*
*I'm going to mess up.*
*They're laughing at me.*
*Everyone's better than me.*
*My coach doesn't like me.*

**Uncomfortable Feelings:**
Anxiety
Fear
Embarrassment
Frustration
Anger

### A Difficult Situation

Think of a difficult roller derby performance situation. Try to recall the situation with as many thoughts, feelings, and details as possible. When you are feeling the same as if you are back in that moment, shift your attention to completing the word search below as quickly as possible.

Find the word, "DIFFICULT." Make sure you check horizontally, vertically, diagonally and even backwards.

Were you able to shift your attention from being in your head and upset to being in the present moment and focused on the task at hand? To be successful at finding the word, "DIFFICULT," what was it necessary for you to focus on? Were your emotions helpful? Were any "what ifs" or self-doubts relevant?

Think about the difficult roller derby performance situation and ask yourself these three questions:
1. What was the roller derby task and how can you tell if you've done it well? This is an exercise in self-awareness. Figure out what you were trying to accomplish.
2. Where has your attention usually been focused during these situations? Typically, for problematic situations, our attention becomes too focused on what is going on inside our head.

3. Where should your attention be focused during the task? Determine what is relevant to focus on for you to be successful.

## A Challenging Situation

Now think of a challenging roller derby performance situation. Again, try to recall the situation as vividly as you possible. As soon as you are feeling the same emotions and thinking the same thoughts as you were that day, shift your attention to completing the activity below as fast as you can.

For each group of letters, spot the "b."

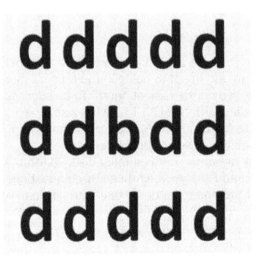

dddddd
ddddddd
dbdddd
ddddddd

dddddddd
ddddddddbd
dddddddddd
dddddddddd
dddddddddd

dddddddddddd
dddddddddddd
dbdddddddddd
dddddddddddd
dddddddddddd
dddddddddddd

ddddddddddddddd
ddddddddddddddd
ddddddddddddddd
ddddddddddddddd
dddddddddbddddd
ddddddddddddddd
ddddddddddddddd

Evaluate how well you were able to shift your attention from negative thoughts and feelings to being fully present and engaged in the task. What were you aware of during the task? What were you thinking and feeling? Now ask yourself the same three questions about the challenging roller derby performance situation:

1. What was the roller derby task and how can you tell if you've done it well?
2. Where has your attention usually been focused during these situations?
3. Where should your attention be focused during the task?

### A Threatening Situation

Last, think of a roller derby performance situation that felt threatening. Use all your senses to immerse yourself in that situation. What were you thinking about? What emotions were you experiencing? Now complete the activity below as quickly as you can.

How many squares are in this picture?

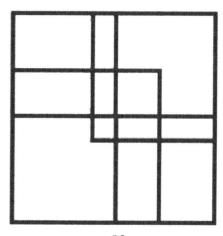

When you are finished, check in with yourself. How easily were you able to shift your attention from the thoughts and feelings related to your threatening situation to the task at hand? What was this exercise like for you? Finally, ask yourself the three questions below:

1. What was the roller derby task and how can you tell if you've done it well?
2. Where has your attention usually been focused during these situations?
3. Where should your attention be focused during the task?

*(Solutions are in the Appendix beginning on page 391.)*

# MENTAL TOUGHNESS TIP #33
## Meet Yourself Where You're At

Too much drive for constant improvement can ruin the appreciation for where you are right now. Don't put your satisfaction and happiness off for the future. Saying, "I will be happy when I'm _____ (faster, stronger, more agile)" can ruin the enjoyment of roller derby.

1. Respect where you've come from.
2. Have your sights set on where you want to go.
3. Appreciate where you're at right now. You are exactly where you should be at this moment.

"I am _____ (fast, strong, agile) enough right now."

4. As you accept that you are "enough" right now, balance that acceptance with an awareness of the areas you want to improve.

*Have the serenity to accept the things I cannot change,*
*The courage to change the things I can,*
*And the wisdom to know the difference*
*-Adapted from the Serenity Prayer by Reinhold Niebuhr*

# MENTAL TOUGHNESS TIP #34
## Flip Negative Thinking

As this *Cognitive Behavioral Triangle* shows, the way we think impacts our emotions and our actions. Thoughts that are unhelpful, negative, or irrational get in the way of our game. Thoughts that are helpful, positive, and rational help us to achieve our top performance.

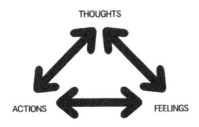

If you think, *I'm not in the mood to practice today*, you will feel things such as boredom, lack of motivation, etc. You likely won't give much effort at practice, essentially being just a warm body. Flipping that unhelpful thought into a helpful one, as shown below, will change how you feel and change your actions.

**Thought:** *I'm here, I'm going to give it my best.*
**Feeling:** Energetic, engaged, motivated
**Action:** Participation in practice

In the space provided, write down a negative, irrational, or unhelpful thought. Indicate how this thought makes you feel and how it influences your actions. Then, flip that thought into a positive, rational, or helpful one that will get you to your derby goals.

Unhelpful Thought: _____

_____

Feeling: _____

Action: _____

**Flip It!**

Helpful Thought: _____

_____

Feeling: _____

Action: _____

# MENTAL TOUGHNESS TIP FOR TEAMS #35
### Give Everyone A Role

Roles are one factor in a strong team. These can be both formal and informal. Formal roles are set by the structure of your organization. These include referees, captains, and coaches. According to sports psychologist, Jean Williams, informal roles that may show up on a team are leader (this may or may not be the captain), enforcer, cop, social director, and clown. It is helpful for everyone on the team to know their role and accept it.

Problems can arise when roles are not clarified or are ambiguous. What is the role of fresh meat on your league? What is the role of a skater in their first game? What is the role of the captain at practices versus at games? A skater who is not the biggest, the fastest, the squirelliest, or the hardest hitting may struggle with defining where they fit in on the team. A coach or other formal or informal leader can help define roles for everyone. Leaders can assign roles to skaters who may not get as much track time during a game. Having a clear part to play will help them not feel left out or confused about their contribution to the team. These skaters can help watch the penalty box, count jammer points, and give feedback to skaters coming off the track. Your team can help give these positions a name (stay away from terms with a negative connotation such as bench warmers or 2nd string).

If skaters don't accept their role, it can be an issue. What happens when your best jammer would rather block? Or when a skater on the team believes they can coach better than the coach? What happens when your personal life affects the role your teammates expect you to play? On a strong team, everyone has a part to play, knows their part, and accepts their part.

Assign everyone a role, even those not rostered due to injury or other reason. This will allow all to own the team's wins and losses. Injured skaters can act as scouts and watch the opposing team for strategies, plays, or skaters that are making an impact. At halftime they can share this information with the team. Fresh meat can provide positive feedback and encouragement to the team.

# MENTAL TOUGHNESS TIP #36
## Know How To Resolve Conflicts

There are clear steps you can take to deal with conflict in a level-headed, effective way. Knowing them will give you the confidence to handle anything the "derbyverse" throws at you.

1. Set the stage. Agree to try to work together to find a solution peacefully. Establish the ground rules. There will be no name calling, blaming, sarcasm, shouting, or interrupting.
2. Gather perspectives. Each skater describes the dispute from their point of view without interruption. Listeners pay close attention and then ask questions in a non-threatening manner to make sure they understand. Listeners consider not only what the other skater wants, but why they want it.
3. Find common values. Figure out which facts or issues all skaters agree on and why different issues are significant to each person. What do you have in common? It may be as simple as a mutual desire to do what is best for the team.
4. Create options. Brainstorm about possible solutions to the problem. Come up with a list of options without immediately judging them or feeling committed to them. Try to think of solutions where all parties gain something—think win-win! Be creative and come up with a solution that all involved feel good about, where everyone walks away feeling like their needs were met.
5. Evaluate options. After several options are suggested, each skater will discuss their thoughts about each. Skaters will then negotiate and will often need to compromise to reach a conclusion that is

acceptable to all. You may need to agree to disagree about some issues to reach an understanding.
6. Create an agreement. Skaters involved will clearly state their agreement and may even want to write it down. If necessary, set up a time to check back to see how the agreement is working.

If you use an approach like this to resolve problems, you will find that conflicts don't have to be avoided and they don't need to lead to drama. Drama occurs when situations that have a fairly easy solution are made unnecessarily complicated by negativity, lying, gossiping, or backstabbing. A lot of social problems can be solved simply by making an effort to help the other person feel heard and understood, responding instead of reacting, and acting according to values rather than emotions.

> *Finding common ground is the only way to bridge differences.*

*(See page 224 for tips on cooling off before confronting teammates.)*

# MENTAL TOUGHNESS TOOL
## BE MINDFUL: BASIC MINDFULNESS EXERCISE

This guided meditation will help you focus on the immediate moment and develop the skill of mindful attention.

Find a comfortable seat. Allow your eyes to close gently or soften your gaze. Breathe in and out gently and deeply several times. Notice the sound and feel of your own breath as you inhale and exhale.

At this time focus your attention on your surroundings. Notice any sounds that you can hear. What sounds do you hear inside the room? What sounds do you hear outside the room? Now focus your attention on the areas where your body touches the surface on which you are sitting. Notice the physical sensations that occur from this contact. Notice any sensations that may be occurring in the rest of your body and notice how they may change over time without any effort on your part. Don't try to alter these sensations, just notice them as they happen.

Let your attention come to your thoughts. Simply observe your thoughts without doing anything to change them. Don't try to make them go away or change them in any way. Notice how they change on their own without you having to do anything.

Remain comfortable for a few more moments and slowly let yourself focus once again on any sounds occurring around you. Once again notice your own breathing. When you are ready, open your eyes and notice that you feel focused and attentive.

# MENTAL TOUGHNESS TIP #37
**Feedback Is Your Friend**

Feedback can be informal or formal. Informal feedback is usually verbal and occurs casually on a daily basis. Formal feedback is typically written and may be part of a planned, scheduled event such as skills testing or tryouts. Appropriate feedback enables athletes to think about the gap between actual and desired performance and helps them identify ways to narrow the gap and improve. Feedback aims to bring a skater's performance to a higher level by dealing with deficits in a constructive way.

If we do not get feedback, this will come with a cost. Skaters may assume that everything is fine and will continue practicing in the same way. This leads them to have a false assessment of their own skills and abilities. But feedback can be difficult for skaters to hear and take to heart. Here are some barriers to effective feedback:

- Generalized feedback not related to specific facts
- Fear of upsetting the person receiving feedback
- Lack of advice on how to improve skills
- A lack of respect for the source of feedback
- Fear of damaging personal relationships
- Defensive behavior/resistance when receiving feedback
- Physical barriers such as noise, or improper time or place
- Personal agendas
- Feedback given in a condescending manner

- Lack of confidence or assertiveness on the part of the person giving feedback

Here are some tips for receiving feedback:
- Be a good listener
- When in doubt, ask for clarification
- Embrace it as a learning opportunity
- Pause and think before responding
- Show an investment in the learning process and that you want to improve
- Be open to helpful hints
- Learn from your mistakes and be motivated
- Have a positive attitude and show appreciation

Being able to receive effective feedback is closely linked to improving your performance. Feedback should be constructive by focusing on specific things that can be improved. Having strong relationships with those giving you feedback will help reduce barriers to both the giving and receiving of constructive feedback and will act as a powerful motivator for athletes to take the feedback to heart.

*"Feedback is the breakfast of champions."*
*-Ken Blanchard*

# MENTAL TOUGHNESS TIP #38
## Awaken Your Senses

Of our five senses—sight, hearing, touch, smell, and taste—it is our eyes that we use the most. We perceive 80% of our impressions from our sense of sight. It is our eyes that allow us to see danger and opportunity on the track. Since we rely so heavily on our sense of sight our other senses don't get used that much. The comic book hero, Daredevil, is blind, but his opponents wouldn't know that because his other senses have developed to superhuman sensitivity. Imagine what it would be like to engage all your senses into your game? Would you experience a heightened level of performance? Try the activity below to awaken your other senses.

### Blind Skate
This activity requires a partner, blindfold, and some obstacles.
1. One person will wear a blindfold and be guided. The other person will be the guide.
2. Lay out some obstacles around the track such as cones, water bottles, shoes—whatever you have on hand. Make sure there is enough room to skate around the obstacles.
3. The blindfolded skater will hold out their hand and the guide will pull them safely around the obstacles, returning them to the starting position where they will switch roles. No talking allowed!
4. As the blindfolded skater, what were you aware of? Discuss what the experience felt like as both the "blind" skater and the guide.

# MENTAL TOUGHNESS TIP #39
**Recognize Your Well Dones**

Keep a derby journal in your gear bag and after every practice and every game, write down three things you did well. Your mind will naturally gravitate toward areas where you are falling short, so you must put a concentrated effort into noticing where you are succeeding. Force your mind to pay attention to what you are doing well, no matter how small. This will increase the likelihood that you will do well in the future.

# MENTAL TOUGHNESS TOOL
## BE FLEXIBLE: HALF LORD OF THE FISHES POSE

A flexible mind and a flexible spine go together. Can what is twisted always be untwisted? Ideas held stubbornly will make untwisting harder because of pride. This book may have many concepts that are new for you. It takes flexibility to give up old ways of doing things and to try something different.

Start by sitting on the earth with your legs straight out in front of you. Bend your knees, put your feet on the earth, and then slide your left foot under your right leg to the outside of your right hip. Lay the outside of the left leg on the earth. The sole of the right foot remains firmly rooted down, with the right knee pointing toward the sky. Press the right hand against the earth behind you. Inhale, and as you exhale, twist toward the inside of the right thigh. Wrap your left arm around your right knee. Let the twisting come from your core rather than trying to force the twist by pulling or pushing with your arms. Lift and lengthen your torso with every inhale and twist a little more with every exhale. Look over your right shoulder if it feels comfortable. Hold for five breaths. Release to your starting point with an inhalation and repeat on the other side.

While you hold this pose, you may find it helpful to reflect on the following:
1. How flexible do I want to be in changing old ways?
2. Is there anything I need to undo?
3. Think of times when a twist of events turned out for the best.

# MENTAL TOUGHNESS TIP #40
**Practice Tapas**

*Tapas*, like most Sanskrit words, means many things to many people. Most simply, tapas is heat. Specifically, it is the kind of heat that comes from certain physical and mental activities, or a certain approach to life.

Tapas means doing something you do not want to do or not doing something you want to do that will have a positive effect on your life. Tapas should be something simple and small enough that you can become successful at it but should also be difficult and challenging enough to engage your will.

Tapas is the friction generated by going against the grain of habit, of complacency, of doing what's easiest, of getting away with things. Tapas is the passion of striving to be the best you can, which may mean shifting what you do and how you do it.

Tapas is self-discipline. Which raises the question of why you are involved in roller derby at all. What is your intention? The Buddhists talk about right thinking and right action. Right effort is not necessarily the same as more effort. You must put your focus on the things that are going to be effective at improving your game and enjoyment of the sport. Look at the ways you can become a better roller derby player and raise the bar of your intention.

Tapas is a personal practice, it is one of Patanjali's five niyamas, or personal observances in yogic tradition. Tapas is a great tool for mental toughness. What is tapas for you? How can you light up your fire? Genuine tapas can make you shine like the sun.

# MENTAL TOUGHNESS TIP #41
## Come Back Strong After An Injury

Some skaters return to bouting following an injury confidently and without any worries. For others, returning to competitive levels of play following a major injury can create incredible stress. Despite being medically cleared, some skaters are just not ready to return psychologically. This tip can help skaters who intend to return to play following a significant injury.

How a skater responds to an injury is determined more from how they interpret or perceive the injury than from the injury itself. Many factors can influence a skater's perception of their injury.

Has the skater come back from an injury before? If not, they may be more stressed as this is new territory. How much of an investment does the skater have in roller derby? For those who have achieved success and are intensely involved, the whole focus of their identity, their sense of who they are as people, may be tied up in the role of athlete. For those, an injury can feel devastating.

A skater who is stressed and lacks confidence when returning to competition will be more prone to re-injury. It creates a self-fulfilling prophecy. If you think you will get hurt, you probably will. The fear of injury causes you to play with rigidity and caution. You won't be participating with the commitment, freedom, and intensity that the circumstances demand. If your head is not 100% in the game, then you are more likely to be injured.

How coaches and teammates react is significant. Old school attitudes about toughness in sports (always give 110% and toughen up, buttercup) can cause injury and failure when taken to extremes. Many highly driven derby participants learn to withstand any amount or kind of pain. This makes for a tough skater but can also make for an often-injured skater who never plays in a fully healthy state. That can lead to a short-lived career and a lifetime of pain.

Coaches and teammates must also avoid giving skaters the message that they are only valuable when they are able to bout. Injured skaters should not be isolated from healthy skaters at practices or games.

Skaters should not be made to feel guilty for not helping their team to win. They should not be made to feel ashamed of being injured or that injuries are something to hide. Skaters shouldn't feel pressured by coaches or teammates to return before they are medically ready.

Coaches and teammates should allow skaters the normal expression of feelings that go along with being injured. They should avoid telling skaters to "cheer up" or "it's going to be fine." Grieving is an essential and necessary part of the recovery process. The must avoid treating the skater as the injury. A skater is just as much of an athlete, just as much of a person, as before the injury.

Be aware of the potential for internal conflict among teammates. They may stay away from the injured skater because they represent a threat of injury to themselves. Teammates may think, "If it can happen to them, it can happen to me." This can be more of a problem if an injury is particularly gruesome or visible. The injury of one skater may present another skater on the team the opportunity to shine. Teammates may have mixed feelings when giving injured skaters emotional support and wishes for a speedy return. Some level of competition is necessary and healthy within a team; however, it should not ever become personal.

The stronger the skater's identification as an athlete, the more their friends and family may have come to interact with them primarily through this role. People may not know quite how to relate to you now—through your past glory or your possible future, not the injured present. Be aware of these potential problems and keep the lines of communication open to prevent an uncomfortable situation.

What can you do to come back confident and stress free following an injury?

1. Get back to practice! You should rejoin the team as soon as humanly possible, even on crutches or bandaged. When you are away from your team for a length of time you may feel that your team has moved on without you. There may be new jokes, new team members, etc. By being there, you will grow and develop along with your team. Find ways to be involved. For example, you can observe a teammate who plays a similar position and give feedback while mentally engaging in the activities.
2. Use a peer mentor. Talk to a skater who has successfully rehabilitated and returned from a similar injury. They can give you tips on what helped or hindered their progress.
3. Separate discomfort from injury. Learn to differentiate between discomfort and injury, pressure and damage. Some discomfort is a normal part of muscle exertion, damage is not.
4. Look for the silver lining. It can be helpful to develop positive meaning from the injury. Some athletes have come out of injuries with better/smarter technical skating, increased mental toughness, and clearer

priorities. Being injured and recovering, living through it, can teach us that we are stronger than we thought we were. It can show us how much we can endure. Living through an injury can reduce fear of future injuries because we know that we are strong and can heal.

5. Be sad. Understand reasonable responses to an injury. It is normal to feel frustrated and disappointed with your progress. It is not reasonable to feel hopeless, that the injury is a sign of weakness, or to assume that your derby career is over.

6. Be informed. Learn about the injury itself and the rehabilitation process. Lacking knowledge can increase anxiety.

7. Use imagery. Visualize returning to competition and kicking ass confidently and without fear of injury. We tend to imagine the worst that could happen. Instead, imagine situations that bring on feelings of pride, accomplishment, enthusiasm and confidence.

8. Set goals. Collaborate with your coaches on short- and long-term goals. For example:

    a) "I will skate 10 laps today."

    b) "By the end of the month I will scrimmage in three jams."

    c) "I will skate in our July game."

Goal setting will increase your commitment to fully returning to competitive play. As you accomplish goals without injury you will feel successful and your confidence will grow.

9. Practice relaxation. Playing while rigid or anticipating pain/injury is dangerous and will lead to re-injury. Also, tensions in the injured area can increase pain and work against the effectiveness of rehabilitation.

Ultimately, the decision to continue to skate following an injury is an individual choice. Every skater must do their own cost/benefit analysis. Whether it is the thrill of competition, the fitness, the friendships, the status... whatever...the payoff must be worth it for *you*.

*Once you play roller derby everything else is easy.*

(See page 239 for a progressive muscle relaxation.)

# MENTAL TOUGHNESS TIP #42
## Use The Power of "Yet"

"I'll never be able to do that."
"I can't do that yet."

The first statement above is indicative of a person who is stuck in the now. This person can't see a future that is different from today. The second statement is full of change, possibility, and dreams. The two statements demonstrate the difference between a fixed mindset and a growth mindset. Brain scans show a difference in people experiencing these two states of mind. An engaged, fired up brain can be seen in those who are in "yet." Individuals who are stuck in the now have brains that are shut down and non-engaged. Using "yet" shows the world and yourself that you can get there with work and time.

Using "yet" gives a person:
- Effort
- Determination
- Strategy
- Perseverance
- Grit
- Resilience

The experience of effort and difficulty must be reinterpreted. For people in a now mindset, those feelings make them think they are incompetent. For individuals in a "yet" mindset, those feelings indicate growth and change. Listen to the words you use when confronted with a challenge.

Be sure to end any statement with the word "yet":
- "I haven't tried that yet."
- "I'm not that fast yet."
- "I can't stop them yet."
- "I'm not ready for that yet."
- "I'm not brave enough yet."

Don't give up. Stay focused and determined and you'll get there. The powerful word, "yet," gives you greater confidence and a path out of your comfort zone and into the future.

# MENTAL TOUGHNESS TIP #43
## Honor All Emotions

It is key to accept and honor all emotions, even if they are conflicting. Think of a roller derby situation in which you experienced two conflicting emotions. Write the situation and two feelings down below. If you only listened to one of the feelings, what action would that lead to? Finally, come up with a way to honor both emotions.

Situation: _____

_____

**Feeling #1:** _____

If I only listen to this feeling, I will:

_____

**Feeling #2:** _____

If I only listen to this feeling, I will:

_____

I can honor both feelings by: _____

_____

What would life be like if we only listened to fear or any other single feeling? By honoring all emotions, you can make balanced decisions you can feel good about.

# MENTAL TOUGHNESS TOOL
## BE POSITIVE: PUT YOUR DERBY NAME INTO ACTION

Write down your roller derby name and think of a positive, action-oriented word for each letter. Select words that you identify with, want to be, and that you can translate into actions. A few ideas for each letter are provided below. What can you do and say every day to *be* these words?

**A:** Assertive, Authentic, Attentive
**B**: Balanced, Blissful, Bonafide
**C:** Calm, Consistent, Cheerful
**D:** Devoted, Disciplined, Dependable
**E:** Enthusiastic, Excited, Energetic
**F:** Fearless, Focused, Forgiving
**G:** Generous, Grateful, Giggly
**H:** Happy, Humble, Honest
**I:** Inspirational, Invincible, Involved
**J:** Joyous, Just, Joker
**K:** Kind, Knowledgeable, Killer
**L:** Loving, Loyal, Leader
**M:** Majestic, Mellow, Motivational
**N:** Nurturing, Nice, Noteworthy
**O:** Optimistic, Open, Original
**P:** Positive, Proud, Powerful
**Q:** Quiet, Quality, Quick
**R:** Relaxed, Resilient, Regal
**S**: Spontaneous, Sweet, Supercharged
**T:** Trusting, Tolerant, Triumphant
**U:** Unique, Understanding, Unlimited
**V:** Valuable, Virtuous, Vibrant
**W:** Worthy, Wondrous, Wise

**X:** Xenial, X-Ray Visionary, X-Factor
**Y:** Youthful, Yearner
**Z:** Zany, Zippy, Zealous


My roller derby name:

_____


My words of positivity and action:

_____


_____


_____


_____


_____

## MENTAL TOUGHNESS TIP #44
**Maximize Your Chances Of Being In The Zone**

Have you heard of *The Zone?* This is the legendary experience athletes have when they feel like they are playing their absolute best.

When you are in The Zone:
- You are completely immersed in what you are doing
- You have a feeling of being outside everyday reality
- There is a clear understanding of what you want to achieve
- You aren't aware of being tired or sore
- You have confidence that you can handle the task at hand
- There is a sense of timelessness
- You're not worried about yourself
- There is a match between your skill level and the challenge
- You're not thinking about what your body is doing
- Your actions feel effortless

According to positive psychologist, Mihaly Csikszentmihalyi, in this *flow state,* "your whole being is involved, and you're using your skills to the utmost." To increase your chances of playing in the zone, practice mindfulness, become self-aware, focus on what is relevant, be in-the-moment, and build your confidence. Identify the areas in which you need to build your mental toughness, create a plan for improvement, and flow!

# MENTAL TOUGHNESS TIP #45
## Take Concussions Seriously

As the 2015 movie, *Concussion*, dramatically showed, a sport's ethics and culture are linked to the occurrence of injury. Athletes will internalize beliefs that being tough means playing with pain and injury and that pain and injury are normal and expected. From a sociological perspective, injury risk increases the more a sport's culture defines success in narrow terms of wins and losses rather than intrinsic motivation for achievement (enjoyment of an activity for its own sake). Roller derby, like other sports (especially full contact sports), cultivates a culture of risk.

Mottos such as "Go big or go home" and "Winners never quit" give the message that athletes should play through pain and injury for the sake of a win. The disturbing impact of this culture is seen in the recent focus on concussions. Many athletes who play full contact sports state they suffered multiple concussions during their careers but still went back in and continued playing.

While there are no statistics about the frequency of concussions in roller derby, there is a frightening body of evidence showing concussions are incredibly common in American football. In the early 2000s the first National Football League (NFL) player was diagnosed with chronic traumatic encephalopathy (CTE). Since that time doctors have learned a lot about concussions and CTE, which is a degenerative brain condition believed to be caused by repeated impacts to the brain.

When you hit your head hard, your brain can bounce around in your skull causing the traumatic brain injury known as a concussion. Concussion can also occur without hitting your head. Impacts to the body, which occur frequently in our sport, can cause a whiplash-like movement of the head which may generate high enough accelerations to cause brain injury. When the brain experiences a concussion, individual neurons can be stretched and damaged making people "see stars," become disoriented, pass out, become sensitive to light and sound, experience headaches, and have slow thoughts for weeks and even months. Some NFL players have shown alarming psychological reactions such as cognitive deficits, severe depression, and suicide. Deterioration of brain functioning happens even after retiring from football.

Roller derby participants receive jarring hits multiple times per week during practice. Even if those hits don't cause damage that reaches the threshold of a concussion, they can still lead to lasting structural changes in the brain. The best evidence says it is these "subconcussive" impacts that are the actual driving force behind CTE, not concussions. Unfortunately, the only way to diagnose CTE is in an autopsy. In 2017, the *Journal of the American Medical Association* published disturbing findings that showed 99% of the brains that had been donated to medical research by former NFL players had CTE. And the longer they had played, the worse their condition was.

Roller derby, like football, is a full contact sport involving bodies colliding into one another and impacting against the skating surface (often unforgiving concrete). We have anecdotal evidence that concussions are all too common and subconcussive impacts occur regularly. How many times have you or skaters you know experienced a concussion or minor jolt to the brain during practice or play?

It is difficult to know what this growing body of knowledge means for the future of roller derby. Concussion and CTE research as related to sports is in its developmental stages. There is much to be learned about cause and prevention models. The Women's Flat Track Derby Association (WFTDA) provides us with robust assessment and return-to-play guidelines, rules established with skater safety in mind, and helmet requirements, but concussion reduction information is limited.

As the WFTDA Risk Management Guidelines (2018) state, "Concussions...will occur in roller derby." There is no way to avoid them without drastically changing the nature of our sport. Below are some things to consider which may reduce concussions in roller derby.

1. Monitor concussions much more closely and take precautions with players who have had more than one concussion.
2. Seek out softer skating surfaces.
3. Vision training to improve peripheral vision (see page 281 for information on how to do this).
4. Limit contact time at practices. Currently there is no evidence available that provides a scientific basis for implementing a specific limit on the number of impacts or the magnitude of impacts per week or per season. However, limiting the repetitions to the minimum necessary to achieve particular learning points is a great way to prevent needless injury. A thoughtful approach to drills and practices can go a long way!
5. Use helmets rated for multiple impacts. Many helmets are only rated for a single impact and then are

meant to be replaced. But how often are skaters really doing that?
6. Consider expulsion warnings for blocks to the head or with the head.
7. More focus on fall-training.
8. Provide regular baseline concussion assessment for skaters.
9. Delay the introduction of contact by disallowing body checking in ages under 13. Evidence shows CTE in NFL players was more pronounced in those who began participating in full contact before age 12.

The purpose of this tip and these harm reduction suggestions is to spark more conversations in the roller derby community about the serious nature of concussions and CTE. As the Consensus Statement on Concussion in Sport from the British Journal of Sports Medicine states, "psychological and sociocultural factors in sport play a significant role in the uptake of any injury-prevention strategy and require consideration."

# MENTAL TOUGHNESS TIP #46
## Defuse From Your Thoughts

The word fusion means things are joined together to form one. Cognitive has to do with the stuff going on in our head such as thoughts, attitudes, ideas, and beliefs. Therefore, *cognitive fusion* refers to us becoming too focused on what is going on in our head. When we experience cognitive fusion, we make decisions based on our internal experiences rather than on what is really going on around us. This can become a barrier when we treat our thoughts like they are absolute truths or as if they are a command we must follow. Our thoughts end up running our lives.

Cognitive defusion is the opposite of this. When we are defused from our thoughts, we can observe them objectively and see them for what they really are—just stuff our mind is telling us.

Thoughts:
- May or may not be true
- Are not a command you have to obey
- Are not a threat to you
- Are not something happening in the physical realm
- Can be allowed to come and go on their own
- Don't have to be controlled or avoided

There should be a difference between reacting to a real event and thinking about such an event. This may seem obvious, but the way humans are designed, we have the same emotional, cognitive, and physical reactions whether an event is real or imaginary. This causes us to be emotionally and physically responsive to our thoughts. We become fused with them.

As an example of this phenomenon, pay attention to your very real sensory responses when thinking about peeling an orange:

### Peeling An Orange

Imagine you are holding an orange in your hands. See the bright color, feel the bumpy texture of the orange's skin and imagine squeezing the fruit with your fingers. Now imagine peeling the orange by digging your thumb beneath the surface of the skin. Imagine your fingers and thumb working to remove the outer layer of the fruit. Feel the sweet and tangy spray as the juice begins to run onto your hand. Try to imagine the distinctive aroma. Once you have fully peeled the orange, picture yourself dividing it into segments before eating it. Recall the taste of the fruit as vividly as you can.

Mindfulness practice allows us to take a spectator's view of our thoughts. It lets us differentiate between what is real and what our mind *tells us* is real. To defuse from your thoughts, practice mindfulness exercises such as the simple practice on the following page which gives an immediate experience of mindfulness of thought.

It is said, as soon as you notice a thought, it disappears! When we are thinking of a thing, we are lost in it. But when we become aware of our thinking, we are in a secondary state, becoming observers of our own thoughts. The actual thinking of the thing is gone and there is either just awareness or we begin a new thought based on that awareness. Either way, the original thinking has vanished.

## Thought Counting Exercise

Get two bowls. One will be empty, and one filled with something you can use as counters such as uncooked beans or buttons. Every time you think a thought you will take one of your counters and place it in the empty bowl. Set a timer for two minutes and get ready to count your thoughts. Thoughts may appear as pictures, images, or words. Thoughts may slow down or speed up. After the time is up, you can count and see how many thoughts you had. Now you know what it is like to directly observe your stream of thoughts.

When you can successfully defuse from your thoughts, they lose their power over you. Thoughts of self-defeat, self-criticism, and negative what-ifs will no longer control you.

# MENTAL TOUGHNESS TIP #47
## Know Perfection Is A Myth

Perfectionism, or the belief that your performance must be just-so to be acceptable, can lead to frustrations, self-doubts, and unhappiness. Perfectionism is an example of "all-or-nothing" or "black and white" thinking which can lead to overly negative views of your performance. Perfectionism is limiting because it only provides two possible outcomes: *I did it* or *I failed.*

The danger in seeking a perfect performance is that it just doesn't exist! Having unrealistic expectations that perfection is achievable will cause you to end up feeling disappointed in yourself. Ideals are meant to inform our training by pointing us in the direction we want to go, fueling our drive to improve. An elite athlete who believes they have achieved perfection, is an athlete who is no longer hungry.

Within each attempt are both areas of success and areas in which to grow. See the shades of grey instead of just black or white. It might help to pick out different aspects of a single skill (e.g. speed, strength, control, outcome, guts) and rate your performance on a scale from 1 to 5 for each. Some of these areas you may be doing pretty well at and others may need work. It's never a total failure or a total triumph.

*Perfection is a direction, not a destination.*

# MENTAL TOUGHNESS TOOL
## BE DRIVEN: GOAL MAPPING

Brian Mayne created a fun goal setting system that uses words and pictures to communicate to both the left and right sides of the brain. Follow his steps below and watch your derby dreams turn into reality.

### Step 1: Dream

Imagine that you have your own magical genie just waiting to help you achieve whatever you really want. Whatever you think about becomes a wish and commands your genie. Close your eyes for a little while and imagine what your ideal roller derby life would be like. Think a big dream full of heartfelt wishes. When you open your eyes, immediately start writing out a list of everything you want to achieve.

## My Wishes

1.

2.

3.

4.

5.

6.

7.

8.

9.

10.

## Step 2: Order

When you are dreaming of the way you would like your roller derby life to be, what stands out as the main goal? Achieving this goal might even help you attain your other goals. Choose the one thing from your list you feel most excited about and write it on the left-brain goal mapping template (reproduced with permission on page 136) in the center box marked 'main-goal.' Write it as if you've already achieved it, such as, "I am skating 30 laps in 5 minutes." Now choose four more wishes from your list and write them in the same way, this time in the boxes marked sub-goals' on either side of your main goal.

## Step 3: Draw

On the right-brain goal mapping template (reproduced with permission on page 138), draw pictures of your goals. Your drawings can be as simple or fancy as you choose. Use lots of color as this really makes your genie take notice. Start by drawing a picture of your main-goal in the center circle and then pictures of your sub-goals on the four branches on either side.

## Step 4: Why

Think now about why you want your goals. What are your strongest reasons and what good feelings does the thought of achieving your goals give you such as happiness, love, and family? Write your reasons in the top boxes of your left-brain template and then draw pictures of your reasons on your right-brain template.

**Brian Mayne's Goal MAPPING** — Left-brain Goal Mapping template for words

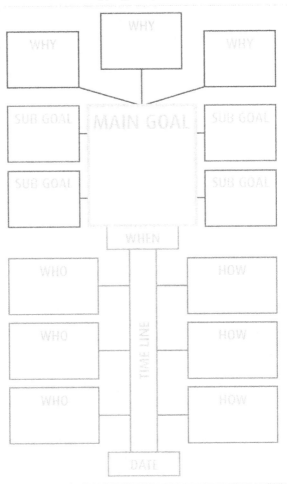

### Step 5: When

Now choose a date for when you want to achieve your goals. You may want your goals straight away, but all genies need a little time to work their magic. What do you think will be a good timeline for you and your genie to achieve your goals? Write the date on both maps in the small circle and box just below your main goal. Now write today's date in the circle and box at the bottom of the page.

### Step 6: How

Next think of some of the things you can do that will help you move toward your goal, such as learning new skills. Once you have thought of some actions you can take, write them in the boxes marked HOW on your left-brain goal template. Then draw pictures on your right-brain goal template. Put the action you can start first on the bottom branch of the trunk with the other actions moving up toward the top.

### Step 7: Who

The last step is to decide who you would like to help you. Depending on what your goal is, it could be a member of your family, a friend, your coach, or a teammate who you would like to help. Write the person's name in the box marked WHO on your left-brain goal map opposite the action you want help with. Then draw pictures on your right-brain goal map.

Finally, sign your goal map and say your goals out loud every morning while looking at the pictures and imagining how it will feel to achieve your greatest roller derby dreams.

# Right-brain Goal Mapping template for pictures

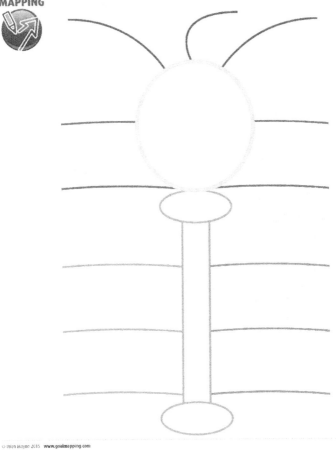

## MENTAL TOUGHNESS TIP #48
### Be Your Best Self

Over time, we build up layers over our true, best, authentic self with doubts, jealousies, insecurities, worries, defenses, mistrust, anger, and fear. But your best self is always inside of you, at your core. Times of stillness and silence allow you access to your best self. Sitting with eyes closed illuminates our inner world, allowing us to see more clearly. To find your best self, sit with eyes closed, silent and still, for two minutes every day.

# MENTAL TOUGHNESS TIP #49
## Practice Radical Acceptance

Radical acceptance means accepting roller derby on roller derby's terms. Radical acceptance is not resisting what you cannot or choose not to change. It is about saying YES to roller derby, just as it is.

Don't try to avoid, control, or eliminate negative thoughts and feelings from your experience. Thoughts and emotions come and go if we let them. Accepting that all kinds of thoughts and feelings will be part of your roller derby journey, from ultimate ecstasy to crushing defeat, will help you act in ways that are true to your values rather than driven by your emotions.

Emotions aren't what is getting in the way of being the best skater you can possibly be. Emotions are not the problem. Reacting to emotions in ways that take you away from your goals is the problem. Emotions, good or bad, are part of this crazy, roller derby roller coaster. Disappointment, excitement, regret, jealousy, embarrassment, rage, happiness, fear, sadness, frustration, joy...these are all a part of it. It is what makes it so amazing! Roller derby can be brutal, mean, and unforgiving. But it is also insanely rewarding. You can't have the mile-high peaks without the deep, dark valleys.

An emotion-driven life means always trying to feel good and avoid feeling bad. When we run away from situations where we might end up feeling bad, we hinder our success as athletes. It is the most adverse, difficult moments that truly define us and where we find the most growth.

If we are avoiding negative feelings, we may do things like:
1. Choose to practice something we are already good at instead of something new so that we feel good about ourselves.
2. Skip practice after a fight with a teammate because we don't want to feel irritated again.
3. Only volunteer to jam when we see the opposing team's blockers are at a lower level than us, so we don't have to feel embarrassed.

These emotion-driven actions keep us from being the best skater we can be. We need to challenge ourselves, attend practice regularly, face fears, and risk feeling badly to advance our skills. Can you think of some situations where trying to make yourself feel good, or avoid feeling bad. caused you to do things that hurt your roller derby career?

Living an emotion-driven life gets in the way of being true to our values. We may act in ways that are inconsistent and don't represent who we really are or what is important to us. Here are some examples:
1. Being unsupportive of a teammate's success because we feel jealous.
2. Acting friendly to fresh meat only on days when we are in a good mood.
3. Saying "thank you" to compliments only when we feel good about our performance and denying them otherwise.

Accept that all kinds of emotions are part of roller derby. This will allow you to act in value-driven ways that will help you achieve your goals.

# MENTAL TOUGHNESS TIP FOR TEAMS #50
## Win With Class, Lose With Grace

Losing can be hard to handle. Some skaters question their talent, blame others, or become depressed or angry. Taking these steps after a loss can help you accept it with grace:

1. Smile. Challenge yourself to go through the same end-of-game rituals no matter what the score outcome is. Whether you win or lose, smile, high five your team, and congratulate the other team.
2. Don't take it personally. Never let the outcome of your performance define who you are as a person. Take a healthy view of adversity and difficulty. Be fully prepared to win the next one!
3. Take time to process the loss but put a time limit on it. For example, "I can have a pity party through the weekend but will focus on the future come Monday."
4. Take a balanced look. There were things you or your team did well. Identify them.
5. Find the lesson. Figure out what you can do to improve for the next game. Losses are opportunities for growth.
6. Put an improvement plan into action. Take the steps to become the skater and team you want to be.
7. Accept that losses will happen. You win some, you lose some.

*"It is one thing to be declared the winner, it is quite another to really win."*
*-Josephson Institute*

Keep the concept of winning and losing in perspective. Wins and losses aren't absolute values. When does winning mean the most?

- You beat a team that is equal to or better than your team
- Your team plays their best

When is a win not as significant?
- You beat a weaker team
- You played dirty to win

When is a loss the most devastating?
- You don't play your best
- You lose against a team that isn't as good as your team

When is losing not so bad?
- You lose to a better team
- Your team plays its best until the very last whistle

When you win a game, do so with class. Gloating, bragging, or putting down the other team (even in private) are not indicative of good sportsmanship. Just as losing doesn't make you a loser as a person, winning doesn't make you a winner. Enjoy your win, you deserved it! But avoid complacency and the idea that you no longer must train hard. It can be challenging for a team on a winning streak to stay humble and hungry. Following every game, win or lose, determine your individual and team strengths and weaknesses. Commit yourself to continual learning and improvement.

# MENTAL TOUGHNESS TOOL
## BE MINDFUL: ROLLER DERBY MINDFULNESS ACTIVITY I

Next time you are at practice, complete a simple roller derby activity that you can easily do without paying much attention. Warm-up laps, pre-practice stretching, or gearing up are all good ideas. In being mindful, you will focus completely on the task instead of not paying attention. Being mindful means your mind and your body are in the same place.

Your goals in completing this activity are to be able to:
1. Observe and describe your thoughts, feelings, and actions.
2. Observe and describe what is going on in your surroundings.
3. Be in the moment.
4. Be nonjudgmental (don't think of anything occurring internally or externally as being good or bad).
5. Notice if your mind drifts away from the task and if it does, gently bring it back.

# MENTAL TOUGHNESS TIP #51
## Take Care of Yourself

When we are in a good place in heart, mind, and body, it puts us in the best position to take on whatever difficulties life throws at us. Make a list of the things you do to be at your emotional, physical, and spiritual best.

1. _____

2. _____

3. _____

4. _____

5. _____

Think of your self-care practices as a foundational, necessary, must-do part of your life. They will help you to be resilient!

# MENTAL TOUGHNESS TIP #52
**Approach Not Avoid**

Fear and anxiety are the top emotions skaters identify as barriers to optimum performance. When working to decrease the power of these emotional barriers, we always want to approach uncomfortable situations rather than avoid them. Otherwise we allow the fear or anxiety to dictate how we live.

Think of something you want to accomplish but fear or anxiety has been holding you back. This could be trying something new at practice, running for team captain, or attempting an apex jump during a game.

Fear and anxiety come from our inner, scary world of "what ifs." These "what ifs" are usually warning against catastrophic outcomes. *What if I fail? What if I let my team down? What if people laugh at me? What if I get hurt?* Our fear or anxiety is trying to protect us from emotional or physical insult or injury. The emotions are alerting us to a potential threat to our system. Our system is protecting us from experiencing a negative emotional or physical outcome. If we avoid taking the action, we are immediately rewarded with relief from the uncomfortable feeling of fear or anxiety.

To accomplish your goals, ride the fear or anxiety by replacing negative, unhelpful "what ifs" with positive, helpful outcomes.

| **Instead of:** | **Think this instead:** |
|---|---|
| *I can't get through.* | *I will get through.* |
| *I can't do this.* | *I can do this.* |
| *We can't stop her.* | *We will stop her.* |

Then act is if this is true. Do this immediately before fear becomes too overwhelming and the executive, thinking part of your brain loses control. Fear can feel like an impenetrable barrier, so it is vital to always move forward through the fear, with the fear, riding the fear like a wave. In this way, feeling fear or anxiety will be your signal that you are about to do something amazing, instead of backing off.

## *Expect success.*

Instead of listening to my negative/unhelpful "what ifs":

1. _____

2. _____

I will ride the fear by focusing on these positive outcomes:

1. _____

2. _____

# MENTAL TOUGHNESS TIP FOR TEAMS #53
**Promote Healthy Body Images**

They say the jammer has the glamour, but that means the jammer also has the added pressures that come from having all eyes on her. *Foundations of Sport and Fitness Psychology* reports female athletes who are in a "performer" position are at higher risk for developing eating disorders. One way to prevent disordered eating for you and your teammates is to ban comments about body size and shape from your practice space. Even casual comments such as, "She has the perfect butt for derby," can create an unhealthy body consciousness.

*Keep the focus on fitness and ability instead of size and shape.*

# MENTAL TOUGHNESS TIP #54
## Soften Your Edges

Yoga can teach us many things we can apply to roller derby and life. One of those things is how to tolerate the discomfort that is part of learning, growing, and changing. To stretch a tight muscle, we should go directly into a pose that stretches and opens that muscle, breathing into it, not around it. We want to always breathe into the discomfort, coexisting with it, rather than avoiding it. If you want to stretch out of your comfort zone in roller derby you need to approach it in the same way, going straight at the area of discomfort, breathing into it, and allowing your emotional and physical edges to expand. This is the way to become more flexible in body and mind.

The seated forward fold pose can help you use yoga as a vehicle for understanding. Sit on the earth with your legs straight out in front of you, feet together. Start by sitting up with spine long, gazing ahead, hands next to your hips in preparation. Next begin walking your hands toward your feet. Lead with your heart, keeping the round out of your back. Your hands may stop at your thighs, calves, feet, or beyond depending on how flexible you are. It is totally okay to bend your knees if needed. Find the place where you feel some stretch, but not too much—the Goldilocks place.

Notice the areas where you feel sensation and send breath into them, telling those areas that everything is cool, everything is fine. Find your physical and mental edge and as you exhale, soften that edge just a little, perhaps folding a tiny bit deeper, even if it is imperceptible to the eye.

## MENTAL TOUGHNESS TOOL
### BE WHOLE: IDENTIFY WHICH EMOTIONS ARE BARRIERS TO YOUR PERFORMANCE

Make a list of the positive and negative emotions you experience in roller derby. Circle the emotions that are barriers to your performance.

| Positive Emotions | Negative Emotions |
|---|---|
| | |

The emotions you circled are barriers because you may do unhelpful things when you try to avoid them or react to them. These actions don't support achieving your roller derby goals. Accept that all emotions, good and bad, are part of the roller derby experience. Selectively numbing ourselves out to certain emotions, will also numb us to their positive counterpart. We can't experience happiness without sadness, fear without courage, or anger without peace.

The emotions that you identify as barriers are the ones to focus on as you build mental toughness. These are the emotions you will need to face and embrace. Listen to them, honor them, see what they have to tell you about the actions you need to take.

# MENTAL TOUGHNESS TIP #55
## Transform By Doing

The first stage of transformation is *knowing*. We know what we need to do to get where we want to be. We know we need to train hard, eat healthy, get adequate sleep, quit smoking, etc. The second stage is *doing* it. The doing/action phase is the toughest stage to stick to. Most people don't make it past this stage because the work gets too hard. For those, their ultimate goals will remain out of reach. The third stage is *becoming*. Once we can put our knowledge into action on a consistent basis, we transform into who we wanted to become.

"I want to" becomes "I am."

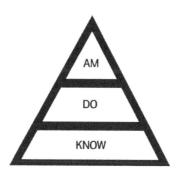

# MENTAL TOUGHNESS TIP #56
## Be Aggressive

It is vital that roller derby participants have an aggressive mindset. This doesn't mean athletes should try to injure their opponents. Aggressiveness in sports is an attitude in which athletes are proactive, assertive, forceful, and hard driving. They take risks, don't give up, and don't hold back.

This aggressive mindset allows athletes to take their performance to the next level, particularly for those who aren't naturally aggressive. An aggressive approach is necessary in a "combat sport" like roller derby. Athletes do battle not only with opposing teams, but also track conditions, and their own emotions. By assuming an aggressive attitude, you have a chance to vanquish these "enemies."

An aggressive mindset can be developed in several ways. First, you're more likely to perform aggressively if your body is amped up. You can raise your physical intensity with more movement during your pre-game warm ups and just before you begin to compete.

Second, you can use high-energy self-talk to instill an aggressive mindset. Examples include, "Fight," "Attack," "Go," and "Bring it!" How you say these words are just as critical as what you say. Make sure your aggressive self-talk sounds like you mean it.

Third, you can use mental imagery in which you see and feel yourself competing aggressively which helps create more attacking thinking, feeling, and doing. What image can you use to focus your aggressive mindset? A hornet, rocket, dragon, firecracker, tank, or cyclone? Be creative!

Write or draw a picture of your image here:

What are the qualities of this image that you want to channel?

_____

What actions do you want this image to inspire?

_____

When you need to be aggressive, combine your image with self-talk and focusing. Let go of all other thoughts except for those that are helpful in this moment. For example, the aggression cue word, "tank" can represent qualities such as strength, invincibility, and intimidation. An action a tank can inspire are launching a menacing attack without hesitation. Visualize yourself as the tank, taking on opposing players, thinking, *I am a tank. Unstoppable. Forward, Forward, Forward.*

# MENTAL TOUGHNESS TOOL
## BE FOCUSED: MAKE A DISTRACTION PLAN

Use the Distraction Plan on the next page to make a list of a few things that distract you during a game. Next to each one, write down what your usual reaction has been in the past. Then note why that reaction has been problematic. How did it hurt your game? Finally, write what your new, desirable response will be and how that will change your game for the better.

Your Distraction Plan can include distractors like:
- Worries about the competition
- Pre-game hassles
- Stressful game scenarios
- Fears of injury
- Disagreements with coach
- Being close to fouling out
- Crabby teammate
- Not feeling well
- Intimidated by opponent

| Distraction | Past Reaction | How this hurt my game | New response | How this will help my game |
|---|---|---|---|---|
|  |  |  |  |  |
|  |  |  |  |  |
|  |  |  |  |  |

# MENTAL TOUGHNESS TIP #57
**Respect Karma**

Karma literally means actions or deeds in Sanskrit. Any intentional action, whether mental, physical, or verbal is Karma. Involuntary, unintentional, or unconscious actions are not Karma because they lack volition. Karma is a law of cause and effect. Every volitional action is eventually accompanied by its due effect. Karma is the action and *Vipaka* is the fruit or the result of that action. The fruition of Karma may be influenced to some extent by external circumstances, surroundings, personality, individual striving, and so forth. But even if we are born into or find ourselves in disparaging circumstances, by our own self-directed efforts there is every possibility for us to create new, favorable environments in the here and now.

Strictly speaking, both Karma and Vipaka pertain to the mind. As Karma may be good or bad, Vipaka may be experienced as happiness, bliss, unhappiness or misery, according to the nature of the original action.

Here are some other things to know about Karma:
1. The results of an action may not appear immediately.
2. The strings connecting an action to a result may be invisible.
3. One negative deed is not offset by a positive deed. Each carries their own results individually.

How does this all apply to mental toughness and roller derby? Karma can give hope, resilience, and moral courage. When the unexpected happens, and you experience difficulties, failures, and misfortune, you must try to pull the weeds and plant useful seeds in their place. Your future is in your own hands.

A believer in the laws of Karma remains enthusiastic, is self-reliant, and believes personal efforts make a difference. Overall, Karma teaches individual responsibility for what happens to us in life. You will reap what you sow. Therefore, if you work hard in your sport and have positive intentions, you will see positive results. Happiness or misery, success or failure, awaits us, depending on Karma.

# MENTAL TOUGHNESS TIP #58
## Develop Your Quiet Eye

It is the last jam of the game and the score varies by only one point! This is anyone's game! In extreme game situations a skater might crumble under the pressure. Develop the skill of the *Quiet Eye* to sharpen your focus instead. This enhanced, visual perception eliminates distractions and gives an athlete single-pointed focus on the task at hand.

The better the skater, the longer and steadier their gaze will be right before and during their strike. Less experienced skaters, on the other hand, will shift their focus around on many different areas of the scene with their focus only staying on each point briefly. A steady, final fixation is the mark of the elite athlete. Quiet Eye researcher, Joan Vickers, states these athletes hold their gaze 62% longer than newbies.

The Quiet Eye can lead to feelings of being in the flow state or Zone, where one feels effortless concentration and the mind is clear of everything except the task at hand. The Quiet Eye also may lead to beneficial physiological changes in the body such as decreased heart rate and increased physical coordination. The Quiet Eye decreases distractions and calms the mind and the body at decisive moments, even under extreme stress.

Fortunately, you can train your Quiet Eye skills and become a more resilient athlete by improving your attentional control and external focus. Quiet Eye training may also improve your performance by making you feel like you have the advantage of psychological control.

1. Find your focal point. Choose something relevant to what you want to achieve next. At the start of a jam, a blocker might choose the star on the opposing jammer's helmet cover. A jammer may use a wide, defocused view that takes in all the opposing blockers, without cueing them to which path they plan to take.
2. Take a breath in, hold it briefly in the back of your throat, then slowly exhale while thinking a focusing cue word such as:

*Now*
*Attack*
*Decide*
*Set*
*Ready*

3. Feel yourself settling in mind and body into this moment, eliminating all distractions, and allowing your natural flow to take over.

*(See page 212 for ways to improve your attentional control, page 207 to improve your external focus, and page 66 to work on your focusing and defocusing networks.)*

# MENTAL TOUGHNESS TIP #59
## Use Your Supports

Knowing you have at least one person in your life that you can trust is the single most significant factor in one's resilience. Who do you have on and off your team that you can lean on in times of adversity and stress? For example, your derby wife can help you after a difficult practice by playing your favorite happy song and taking you to frozen yogurt.

Some of the times you may need support:
- Getting injured
- Not getting picked for a roster
- Failing a minimum skills test
- Disagreement with coach
- Losing a game

Accept help and support when you need it. Have the insight to realize when that is. Sometimes we want to isolate and deal with things independently when there are people who can help us. There is no reason to go through things alone. Using your supports can help you get through tough times faster and with more positive outcomes.

On the following page, list the names of those people in your support network and how they can help you.

| Support Person | How They Can Help Me |
|---|---|

1. _____

2. _____

3. _____

4. _____

5. _____

# MENTAL TOUGHNESS TOOL
## BE FOCUSED: EAGLE POSE

One reason yoga helps us train our focus is because many of the poses require our full attention to pull them off. It is a great way to experience the benefits of having your mind and body in the same place.

Eagles are a symbol of pride, power, and victory. They are birds of prey known for their excellent vision, spotting a snake or a mouse from high above. Eagles are often thought of as the king of the birds.

Stand with feet hip distance apart. Bend your knees slightly. Lift your right leg off the earth and cross it tightly over your left knee. Hug your foot into your shin or hook the toes of your right foot behind your left calf. Bend your arms and hook your left elbow under your right elbow in front of your heart. Point thumbs toward your nose and grab your right palm with your left hand. Your palms will be facing each other. Lift your elbows up and stretch your fingers toward the sky. Find a focal point outside of yourself to help you keep balance. Get an eagle's look of determination in your eye. Hold for five to eight breaths. Repeat on the other side.

Getting into this position can be challenging. You may feel awkward, unsteady, or wrapped like a pretzel. Yet, when this pose is achieved, it is possible to concentrate with an eagle's single-pointedness.

While holding this pose, you can think about the following:
1. What are some words that come to mind when thinking about an eagle?
2. What would it feel like to fly?
3. What am I proud of?

# MENTAL TOUGHNESS TIP #60
## Be Cognitively Flexible

Like a flexible body, a flexible mind can bend. The opposite of flexible thinking is rigid thinking. A person with rigid thinking gets stuck on their ideas. Rigid, one-way-only thinking can be very limiting to an athlete, making problem solving, dealing with unexpected situations, working with others, and achieving goals very difficult. Rigid thinking can cause a person to experience frustration, anger, perfectionism, and irritability due to an incapacity to look at things another way.

A flexible mind allows individuals to effectively solve problems because they can see different elements of a situation and arrive at the best course of action. Cognitive flexibility allows skaters to successfully adapt to the unexpected things that frequently happen on the track without remaining stuck in unhelpful reaction patterns. Someone with flexible thinking works well with teammates and coaches. They can respect diverse viewpoints and collaborate. Flexible thinkers are better able to achieve their goals because they won't fall into the all-or-nothing traps of perfectionism. These skaters can evaluate their performance in a nuanced way that leads to greater satisfaction, confidence, and self-esteem.

An athlete with a flexible mind constantly has new tricks up their sleeve. They are unpredictable game changers. A flexible-minded athlete is not stopped by barriers. They go around, over, under, or through. Where others see problems, a flexible person sees solutions. To become more cognitively flexible, start by asking yourself, *Is there another way?*

# MENTAL TOUGHNESS TIP #61
## Make it OK to Make Mistakes

Skaters often struggle with perfectionism, competitive pressure, and making mistakes. Thinking about what just occurred or worrying about making a mistake prevents skaters from focusing on what is happening in the moment. Read on for some ways to keep mistakes from getting in your head and messing up your game.

1. Accept that mistakes will happen. Mistakes are a part of playing at 100%. If you are trying too hard not to screw up, your focus is on what you don't want to do instead of what you do want to do. Give yourself permission to mess up and you will free yourself to perform at your full potential.
2. Immediately turn failure into success. As soon as possible after making an error, mentally rehearse yourself executing the same skills correctly. Avoid self-judgment or blaming others which disrupts your concentration. Learning is only possible when you make mistakes.
3. Make sure you have support. Getting screamed at, belittled, or punished when you make a mistake is going to make everything worse. Roller derby participants are highly competitive and will already be beating themselves up for what just happened. The message from everyone on the team should be an expectation that mistakes are part of the game. Be sure to learn from every mistake and make the next jam your best jam yet!

# MENTAL TOUGHNESS TIP #62
## Feel Your Emotions

Feelings are the physiological sensations that we *feel* in our bodies such as a fluttering in our chest, a tightness in our throat, queasiness in our belly, heaviness or lightness, heat or cool. We can think about these sensations as the ingredients in a cooking pot. When we experience certain ingredients, or sensations, we name them things like anger, love, fear, sadness, or joy—these are our emotions. Feelings are the physiological sensations in our body. Emotions are what we name these sensations. What are the feelings that mean fear for you?

When you understand your emotions as the sum of physiological sensations, they lose some of their power over you. Tell yourself, *This is just something my mind and body is experiencing.* This is especially essential for emotions such as fear, anger, or jealousy that may be keeping you from being your very best. Noticing and naming what you are feeling in your body can put your emotions in a more helpful context, enabling you to handle them better. This will allow you to gain control over your responses on and off the track.

Think of an emotion you are working with. Take some time to tune in to your experience of this emotion. Where and how do you feel it in your body?

Draw an outline of your body below. Then draw where and how you experience the emotion you are working with in your body. You can use words, pictures and symbols.

# MENTAL TOUGHNESS TIP #63
## Send And Receive The Right Message

All communication problems are two-person problems. Misunderstandings are the fault of both the sender and the receiver. The basic, necessary parts of communication are a sender, a receiver, and a message. Even though this seems simple, there are many ways that communication breaks down.

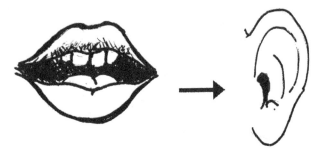

It is imperative that the sender chooses the best way to send a message so that the receiver can understand. You would not send the same message in the same way to a 4-year old, a person who speaks a different language, and your best friend. Common receiving problems include not really listening so you miss vital information, not having the knowledge to understand the message, and adding your own meaning that was not intended by the sender.

*Communication has been effective when the receiver understands what the sender meant to convey.*

Try saying the word, "thanks" in a way that conveys three different meanings:
- Genuinely thankful
- Snarky and sarcastic
- Questioning and not sure

The actual verbal words we use are less important than non-verbal elements of communication for getting our meaning across. 90% of our communication is non-verbal and includes things like body language, facial expressions, and tone of voice.

To avoid miscommunication problems, a receiver can clarify to be sure they have understood the message the sender intended. A sender can confirm with the receiver that the right message was received. Be sure you are sending and receiving the right message. Your team will benefit from effective communication and suffer less drama.

*Responsibility for effective communication falls on both parties.*

# MENTAL TOUGHNESS TOOL
## BE IN CONTROL: CHILL OUT

This mindfulness activity will help you to explore the impermanence of mental and physical discomfort and your emotional response to it.

You'll need:
- A cup with an ice cube
- A napkin to catch drips

1. Hold the cup with the ice cube in it for a few moments. You can start this exercise with a smaller chip of ice and work your way up to a cube. Before you take out the ice, notice the thoughts, emotions and sensations that occur.
2. Take out the piece of ice and hold it in your hand as it melts. Notice any thoughts, emotions and sensations you are having. It may feel uncomfortable to hold the piece of ice, but it won't hurt you. Stay present with the experience (don't daydream or zone out as a way of dealing with it). What thoughts are you having? What are you feeling in your body?
3. If holding the ice is too difficult, put it down for a moment and pick it up again.
4. Notice how the ice feels in your hand as it melts. Does it feel good? Do you want to drop it?
5. As the ice melts, notice how your hand feels. Does the feeling keep changing? What about your thoughts?
6. You can squeeze the ice, shift it to different parts of your hand or move it to your other hand. Notice what happens with each change.
7. How did the feelings in your hand change the longer you held the ice? Did your thoughts change too?

8. Once the ice has melted, you can continue to notice the changing sensations in your hand and the changing thoughts in your mind.
9. If you felt any discomfort during this exercise, how did you handle it?

*"Let the hard things in life break you.*
*Let them effect you.*
*Let them change you.*
*Let those hard moments inform you.*
*Let this pain be your teacher.*
*The experiences of your life are trying to tell you something about yourself.*
*Don't cop out on that.*
*Don't run away and hide under your covers.*
*Lean into it."*
-Pema Chodron

# MENTAL TOUGHNESS TIP FOR TEAMS #64
## Namaste

The word, "Namaste" is commonly heard at the end of a yoga class and may be accompanied by the "anjali mudra" gesture of palms pressed together at the heart center. It literally means, "I bow to you," and is an acknowledgement of the greatness that is in all of us, a commonality that connects us.

Teams that recognize the strength in all its individuals can become more than a mere group of people. They are able to attain a greatness that is more than the sum of its parts. Bringing out each other's strengths, teamwork, and knowing how to make those strengths coalesce are the keys to a winning team.

Here are some ways to bring out the strengths of everyone on your team:

1. Spend time identifying everyone's strengths. Skaters can identify those they feel they have as well as those they see in teammates.
2. Dedicate practice time to reflect on moments when skaters felt they were utilizing their identified strengths.
3. Have skaters also recognize when they see their teammates using their strengths.
4. Determine ways skaters can increase the use of their strengths and how they can also make one another shine.

*Namaste*

## MENTAL TOUGHNESS TOOL
### BE FOCUSED: LION'S BREATH

This breathing exercise calms, centers and focuses the mind and body. You can release any stress and anger you might have by releasing tension when you exhale.

1. Start by sitting on your heels. Alternately, you may crisscross your ankles beneath you.
2. Place your hands on your knees. Straighten your arms and extend your fingers.
3. Inhale through your nose.
4. Exhale strongly through the mouth, making a "haaaa" sound like the roar of a lion. As you exhale, open your mouth wide and stick your tongue as far out as possible, curling it down toward your chin.
5. Try bringing your drishti (focused gaze) toward your Third Eye (center of your forehead) or the tip of your nose as you exhale.
6. Inhale, returning to a neutral facial expression.

Repeat several times. If your ankles are crossed, switch their position so the opposite one is on top half way through your repetitions. This breathing technique makes you look crazy, which could be part of the reason it feels so good.

# MENTAL TOUGHNESS TOOL
## BE SELF-AWARE: MOUNTAIN POSE

A mountain is stable, still, and silent. The mountain can be a symbol of something to overcome or conquer, or perhaps a climb toward a goal you want to achieve. The view from the top of a mountain can be exhilarating but be sure to enjoy the hike to the top as well.

Stand with your feet hip distance apart. Press your feet firmly down into the earth. Your hands can be alongside your body or palms pressed together at heart center. Lift your belly, head, and heart. Your shoulders should be back and down. Look straight ahead, your gaze firm and steady. The muscles in your body are activated. Hold for three to five breaths.

It can be difficult to stand in stillness and silence. However, it is essential to give yourself this time to build an awareness of your mind and body.

As you hold this pose, thinking about these questions may be helpful:
1. What do I stand for?
2. What are my obstacles in life?
3. Am I centered in the present, too impatient, or holding back?

## MENTAL TOUGHNESS TOOL
### BE CENTERED: 5-4-3-2-1 CENTERING EXERCISE

This centering technique will help get you out of your head and grounded in the present moment.

Tune into your environment:
1. What are five things you can see?
2. What are four things you can touch?
3. What are three things you can hear?
4. What are two things you can smell?
5. What is one thing you can taste?

# MENTAL TOUGHNESS TIP #65
## Give Up Attachment To Outcomes

It is not only the ends that matter. Work toward your ultimate goals while also ensuring every step of the way is a win. There are three distinct kinds of goals: performance goals, process goals, and outcome goals. Performance and process goals are the kind you can achieve independent of your opponent. That means these are things you have control over. Setting performance and process goals lets your team have a chance at winning no matter what the scoreboard says.

Performance goals are those you set in relation to your own past performances. Some examples of performance goals are:
- No insubordination penalties
- Pass the star if needed
- Give one assist per jam
- Switch to a defensive jammer when appropriate

Process goals are the actions you need to take to perform well. This is breaking down what it means to be a good roller derby player or team into bite size pieces. Some examples of process goals are:
- Exhale when making a hit
- Stay together with teammates
- Keep an eye on the jammer
- Don't chase the other team

Outcome goals, on the other hand, focus on end results such as winning. According to the Peak Performance Center, outcome goals have been shown to be less effective than performance and process goals in helping athletes or teams reach their optimal level of play. Outcome goals may depend on the actions of others which are not under your control. Setting goals like these sets us up for frustration with the goal setting process. Despite your best effort, an outcome goal may not be achieved. Sometimes you're just outskated. Focusing on outcome goals may suck the pleasure out of the game because it causes skaters to be overly focused on the ends and not enjoy the means. Teams and individual skaters should have performance and process goals going into a game as well as outcome goals. Some examples of outcome goals for individuals and teams follow:

- Win the game
- Be the fastest skater on the team
- Always get lead jammer
- Score 25 points in one jam
- Make it into the championships

Focusing on performance and process goals give you a better sense of control and this builds confidence. Overemphasizing outcome goals can cause anxiety, especially on game day. It is added pressure that you don't need. Outcome goals are great for increasing motivation at practice and helping skaters and teams set long-term goals. However, on game day, set clear performance and process goals.

Cool fact: the more skaters or teams focus on performance and process goals, the more games they end up winning!

*When you play your best it's always a win.*

# MENTAL TOUGHNESS TIP #66
## Plan For Retirement

When should you start planning for retirement from roller derby? The day you start! The topic of retirement can be an emotionally charged one. When asked when they're going to retire, most skaters adamantly say, "Never!" However, at some point even the most dedicated skater's competitive game comes to an end. Reasons for retiring vary from skater to skater and they experience this transition in different ways. For some, it isn't a big deal at all. For others it can be a very upsetting experience.

To make the transition out of competitive play as smooth as possible, plan for retirement before you are ready to retire. Doing this will also help you have a safety net in case you must retire unexpectedly.

**What role will derby play in your life after you retire?** Decide how much involvement in derby you want to have after retirement. Some skaters completely separate themselves from the sport, focusing entirely on other areas of their life. Some continue to be involved as fans. Others consider the derby bonds to be bonds for life and remain close with former teammates. Some skaters may stay active in derby by volunteering, announcing, fundraising, or coaching.

**Respect other parts of your life.** Make sure you have meaningful possibilities to consider when you retire by keeping your life balanced while you are still involved in derby. Maintain non-derby friendships, go to school, hang out with your family, or focus on your career.

**Get your supports ready.** Have the support of at least one close person immediately after you retire. This could be a parent, coach, close friend, teammate, or other loved one. If there are specific ways they can help you, let them know.

**Figure out what's next.** Focus on new areas of interest while you are still competing in derby so that you can jump right into new activities following retirement. Take some classes, try some new sports, or check out some other hobbies. Think of the transition out of competition as a positive opportunity to grow and develop in other directions. Find new ways to get your thrills, maybe without the spills.

**Keep exercising.** Your body is used to a high level of physical activity. You worked hard to get in prime condition so be sure to stay active and keep exercising. It will be good for your mind and your body to stay fit.

**Share your experience with others.** Get together with others who are also going through the retirement transition. Hear about their experiences adapting to a different lifestyle. Too many skaters quit derby and disappear. Think about starting an alumni club!

# MENTAL TOUGHNESS TIP #67
## Beware Of The SHOULDS

The words we use (either out loud or in our head) influence our heart, mind, and body. Certain words shut things down, providing unnecessary rigidity and boundaries. They cause stress because they indicate our attempts to control the uncontrollable. Limit the use of words such as:

Should
Never
Must
Have to
Always
Hate

Replace them with words that indicate possibility, openness, and flexibility of mind, such as:

May
Sometimes
Can
Might
At times
It would be nice if
Prefer

For example, the thought, *I **hate** this drill* can be replaced with, *I **prefer** other drills but that probably means I need this one the most.*

**"Change your thoughts, change your life."**
**-Richard Miller**

*4 wheels move the body,
8 wheels move the soul*

# MENTAL TOUGHNESS TIP #68
## Develop The Vividness Of Your Imagery

The following visualization exercises are adapted from those sports psychologists Robin S. Vealey and Christy A. Greenleaf suggest doing to help you develop the vividness of your mental imagery. For all three exercises, find a comfortable place to sit or lie down. Your eyes can be closed or your gaze softened.

### Vividness Exercise I
In your mind, place yourself in your practice space. It is empty except for you. Stand in the middle of this place and look all around you. Notice the quiet emptiness. Pick out as many details as you can. What are the colors, shapes, and forms that you see? What does it smell like? Now imagine yourself in the same setting, but this time there are many spectators there. Imagine yourself getting ready to play in a game. Try to experience this image from inside your body. See the spectators, the officials, your teammates, your coach, and your opponents. Try to hear the sounds of the crowd, your teammates and opponents talking and yelling, your coach giving instructions, and the sound of wheels on the skating surface. Recreate the feelings of nervous anticipation and excitement that you have before competing. How do you feel?

### Vividness Exercise II
Think about holding your skate in your hands. Try to imagine all the fine details. Turn the skate over in your hands and examine every part of it. Feel its weight, the leather, the laces, the plate, the wheels, and the toe stop.

Now imagine yourself skating around the track. Focus on seeing yourself very clearly skating from behind your own eyes. Visualize yourself repeating the strides over and over. Then step outside of your body and see yourself skating as if you were watching yourself on a video. Now step back into your body and continue skating.

Next try to listen to the sounds of your skates pushing off the floor. Listen carefully to all the sounds involved in your skating. Now put the sight and sound together. Try to get a clear picture of yourself skating and also hearing all the sounds involved.

### Vividness Exercise III

Pick a very simple skating skill. Perform this skill over and over in your mind and imagine every feeling and movement in your muscles as you perform it. Try to feel this image as if you were inside your own body. Concentrate on how the different parts of your body feel as you stretch and contract the various muscles associated with the skill. Think about building a machine as you perform the skill flawlessly over and over again and concentrate on the feeling of the movement.

Now try to combine all your senses, but particularly those of feeling, seeing, and hearing as you imagine yourself performing the skill over and over. Do not concentrate too hard on any one sense. Instead, try to imagine the total experience using all your senses.

# MENTAL TOUGHNESS TOOL
## BE YOUR BEST SELF:
## 14-DAY CHARACTER BUILDING CHALLENGE

To take this 14-day character building challenge, cut out the 14 challenges in the Appendix on pages 395 and 397 and put them into a container. Each day for 14 days, pull one out and put it into action. Watch your character build!

*Stay humble while playing your very best.*

## MENTAL TOUGHNESS TIP #69
### Use Will Power

A lack of determination and discipline can prevent skaters from achieving their goals. Obstacles may arise that make one feel discouraged and want to stop trying. For example, a new skater could look at what a 10-year vet can do and think, *Why even try? I'll never get there!* It is times like this that you need will power to keep you going.

Will power means having the strength of will to keep pushing forward despite wanting to give up. Luckily, if you feel like it is lacking, your will power can be strengthened like the other muscles in your body.

1. Get a friend involved to support and encourage you.
2. Display inspirational photos where you can see them every day to remind you of your dreams.
3. Work on one goal at a time to keep from feeling frustrated and overwhelmed.
4. Remember why you are doing this and what it will cost you if you quit.
5. Anticipate the roadblocks that might keep you from going to practice and be proactive in managing them.
6. While you are working on developing your intrinsic motivation, it is okay to use external rewards. If you do a good job, treat yourself!

*"Strength does not come from physical capacity. It comes from an indomitable will."*
*–Mahatma Gandhi*

# MENTAL TOUGHNESS TIP #70
## Be Here Now

How often are you truly present or immersed in your game? Can you think of a game when you couldn't wait for it to end? Can you think of a game when you couldn't believe it was already over? Those two situations illustrate the difference between being present in the moment and being somewhere else.

If you are not present, you are "time traveling" to the past or future. The past can be filled with all sorts of unpleasant emotions and thoughts such as regret, disappointment, and anger. Thoughts of the future might hold worry, doubt, and fear. Now is all that's real. We can't change the past and we can't predict the future, but we can be fully here *now.*

If we aren't fully present, we can't play our best game. Sometimes we think we are being present, but we are emotionally or cognitively experiencing a "flashback." This happens when we react to a current situation as if it was an upsetting one that happened to us in the past. An example of this is a skater who fouled out in their previous game. This was an extremely distressing event for the skater and they do not want it to happen again. Five minutes into the next game, the skater receives their first penalty. Suddenly they feel as devastated as if they had just fouled out, experiencing the same shock, shame, guilt, and thoughts of letting their team down. The skater is not responding to the current reality where only one penalty has been given. They are responding to what may or may not happen in the future.

To play our best, we need to be 100% fully focused on the present moment. We can't be distracted about what might or might not come next or what already happened in the past. A technique that can help you do this is using your breath as an anchor. Each breath you take is always happening right now so when you focus on your breath you are always here. What follows are some additional strategies for being in the moment.

1. Skate like nobody is watching. This might be a difficult concept to grasp considering roller derby is a team sport played in front of many judging eyes. But imagine the freedom that playing without self-consciousness could bring.
2. Engage. Try to see things with fresh eyes. Avoid going into autopilot. Find one thing to fully immerse yourself in.
3. Flow. Try to forget about time on the clock, penalties logged, or points scored. Get into your groove and play your absolute best.
4. Savor. Instead of worrying about what might happen, find one good thing that is occurring right now. Immerse yourself in it.
5. Accept that whatever just happened can't be changed. It is what it is. Refocus your energy on what you can do *now*.

*Nothing happens next, this is it.*

# MENTAL TOUGHNESS TIP #71
## Imagine Yourself As Your Hero

You are watching a game, and someone takes a big hit. You recoil back thinking, *Ooh that was a bad one!* For a moment it was as if you had been the one to receive the hit, even though you were safely in the stands. This is due to a part of the brain called mirror neurons. These are specialized neurons that activate when we are observing someone doing something. The same parts of your brain will fire as if you are making the movements yourself! Mirror neurons allow us to literally experience what is happening to someone else by observing them.

The implication for sports is we can mentally practice skills without ever lacing up our skates. The brain won't be able to tell if what it is experiencing is real or imaginary.

Think of that skater you fangirl or fanboy about. Choose someone who has skills that you admire and wouldn't mind acquiring for yourself. Find some video clips of the skater in action. While watching the videos, imagine you are that skater. Picture yourself as if you are inhabiting their body. Feel their muscles tense. Sense their contact with other skaters. Join with them in their experience.

The next time you go to practice, your brain will be prepared to take your game to the next level.

*What fires together, wires together.*

# MENTAL TOUGHNESS TIP #72
## Focus On Results

If our attention is focused outside our body on what we want to accomplish, our movement and motor learning will be better controlled. In the science of motor learning (how we learn to make our bodies do the movements necessary to complete a task), there are two categories of knowledge: *Knowledge of Performance* and *Knowledge of Results*. This knowledge comes from feedback that is *intrinsic* (what we learn ourselves from executing the movements) and *augmented* (e.g. feedback from coaches).

Knowledge of performance involves subjective feedback about the mechanics of our movements such as, "You need to bend your knees" and "I need to use my edges more." If our movements are within the parameters of safety and rules, we can concern ourselves less with what it looks like. Too much augmented Knowledge of Performance interferes with the learning process. Our learning system is designed to adapt to achieving the desired results.

Knowledge of Results is objective. It is only concerned with the outcome of the movements. The outcome is either achieved or it isn't. For roller derby this would mean things like:
- Knocking someone out of bounds
- Jumping over an obstacle
- Passing a skater's hips to get their point

If the movements are safe and don't break the rules, who cares what it looks like? Focus on the external results you want to achieve, and your body's learning of the necessary movements will follow.

When practicing, think about what outcome you want to achieve:
*Hit her out*
*Clear this obstacle*
*Get past this skater*

However, don't completely disregard the coach's feedback. Part of their role is to ensure skaters don't injure themselves and that they are executing movements in the most efficient way. But overinsistence on perfect execution of movement during practice can cause a disruption in the motor learning process. Coaches should design drills that build efficient, foundational movements and only stop unsafe attempts. Our motor learning system works best when we allow a natural flow. Start with the goal or the outcome and work backwards, letting the body organize itself. Go with the flow, allow yourself the freedom to experiment, and watch yourself grow.

# MENTAL TOUGHNESS TIP FOR TEAMS #73
## Keep Emotional Tanks Filled

When your team's emotional tanks are filled, they play better. Your teammates will be more open to improvement, show more optimism, deal better with adversity, have more energy, and respond better to challenges.

Unfortunately, we are better at draining tanks than filling them, often doing it without even realizing it. Criticism and sarcasm are drastic tank drainers. Nonverbal actions like frowning, eye rolling, ignoring, and sighing also drain tanks.

According to the Positive Coaching Alliance, if athletes get about five tank-fillers for each criticism, it will lead to optimum performance. Negative interactions bear more weight than positive ones and it takes more than one to undo the damage of one. This 5:1 ratio is called the "Magic Ratio" because it works so well it seems like magic. Here are some tools from *The Power of Double-Goal Coaching* guaranteed to fill those emotional tanks and make your team ready to bring their "A" game.

**Names.** People like hearing their own names so make a point of using your teammates' names often.

**Offer Help.** Offering your help to a teammate is a great way to fill their tank.

**Comings and Goings.** Greet teammates and say goodbye after practices and games.

**Praise.** Keep this genuine and specific. You can tell them when you see them do something well, or when you see them giving maximum effort, even if it doesn't completely go their way. You can also tell teammates when you see them improving. This will keep them trying hard.

**Say Thank You.** Expressing appreciation keeps those tanks filled.

**Notice the Glue.** Be the person on your team who notices and brings attention to the unsung things a person does to hold the team together.

**Check-ins.** Look out for teammates who seem down and ask them how they are doing.

**Asking and Listening.** Asking a teammate for some help or advice and then listening to it is a great way to fill a tank.

**Mistake Ritual.** Your teammates' tanks will be the lowest after making a mistake. Create a positive mistake ritual to make it ok.
   a) Say, "Flush it!" and make a flushing motion.
   b) Say, "Brush it off" and brush yourself off.
   c) Say, "Let it go" and release it.

**Nonverbals.** There are lots of simple ways to keep your teammates' emotional tanks filled such as fist bumps, high fives, head nods, thumbs up, eye contact, smiling, and clapping.

Here are a few more ideas:
1. Invite a teammate you don't know well out for lunch.
2. Go out of your way to look for teammates who need extra tank filling.
3. Send tank-filling messages via texts or social media.
4. Learn the kinds of things that fill your own emotional tank and do them regularly. When your tank is filled you will be in a better position to fill your teammates' tanks.

Try to avoid draining each other's tanks. If your teammates make mistakes, they usually know it, and already feel badly about it. If you criticize them for mistakes, you will make them feel worse, and they might be more likely to make more mistakes.

You can institute a buddy system at some practices. Two skaters will be responsible for watching one another and noticing what the other is doing well. At the end of practice everyone can circle up and share what they saw with the group. This will fill everyone's emotional tanks!

*Use the Magic Ratio of 5:1,
giving five positives for each criticism.*

(See page 222 for more on resetting and letting go in between jams.)

# MENTAL TOUGHNESS TIP FOR TEAMS #74
## Create A Positive Practice Space

What do you want your practice space to be like? What kind of attitudes, energy, effort, emotion, and support are necessary for everyone to be successful? Here are some essential parts of a practice space where all skaters can grow in a positive, safe environment:

**Everyone gets a fair go.** From the newest newb to the most enduring vet, everyone gets their shot at fulfilling their potential.

**Make it safe to screw up.** Fear of making a mistake will limit a skater's learning because they will hold back, not giving 100%. Skaters must receive the message that messing up is ok and a necessary part of the learning process.

**Have the same expectations for everyone.** If your league has practice rules such as no profanity or everyone participates, make sure the rules don't only apply to certain skaters.

Think about your favorite practices. What made them so great? What can you do to create that kind of vibe more often? Are *you* being supportive, focused, energetic, patient, and accepting? Don't take part in a hate/blame game.

*Let positive change start with you!*

# MENTAL TOUGHNESS TIP #75
**Use Your Wise Mind**

Use your Wise Mind to approach emotionally charged situations in a balanced way. Our *Wise Mind* is the place where our reasonable mind and our emotional mind overlap. It is from this place that we do our most balanced and intuitive thinking.

The concept of Wise Mind comes from the world of Dialectical Behavior Therapy (DBT). As the creator of DBT, Marsha Linehan states, "Wise mind is that part of each person that can know and experience truth. It is almost always quiet. It has a certain peace. It is where the person knows something in a centered way."

When we are coming from the place of our emotional mind we will be more reactionary. Our feelings and immediate psychological needs will be the basis for our decisions. When we are in our reasonable mind we use logic, facts, and past experiences to help guide us. If you are a fan of Star Trek, it might be helpful to think of your reasonable mind as your "Vulcan mind" and your emotional mind as your "Captain Kirk mind." When we can come from our Wise Mind, we get to synthesize both worlds and find our truth.

Think of a recent emotionally charged roller derby situation. In the Emotion Mind circle on the following page, write or draw the emotional thoughts, feelings, and urges you had. In the Rational Mind circle, write or draw any facts, logic, or experiences that should be considered. Finally, in the Wise Mind space, write or draw a balanced response or conclusion that honors both sides.

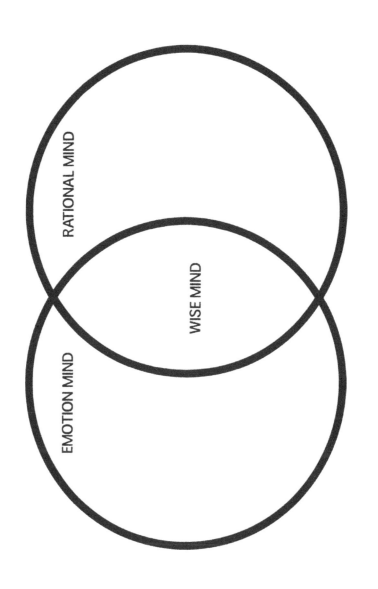

# MENTAL TOUGHNESS TIP #76
## Tolerate Distress

To be poised, an athlete must be able to tolerate all the negative thoughts, emotions, and feelings that go along with being involved in competitive sports. You must be able to play well regardless of what is going on in your head.

Think of a stressful or difficult derby situation you experienced recently. Did you go to the box during a game-deciding last jam? Did you receive an illegal hit? Did you get called a bitch? Did you witness a serious injury? Did the coach yell at you? Really put yourself back in that situation. Take your time. Notice the effect this thinking has on your body and mind. You may feel frustration, fear, anger, sadness, self-blame, a racing heart, or an upset stomach.

Most of us want to escape from these uncomfortable feelings or thoughts. We avoid them at all costs and when they do happen we try to make them go away. That is not always possible. We need to be able to play our best no matter how we are thinking or feeling. Accept that this kind of emotional distress is going to happen. An athlete must channel their energy into their performance rather than trying to change their thoughts and feelings.

Let's go back again to your stressful or difficult roller derby situation. Imagine you are back in that situation. What are you thinking? What is going on for you emotionally and physically. This time sit with any upsetting thoughts, emotions, or uncomfortable physiological sensations without trying to change them or make them go away. You may notice they go away on their own. You don't have to do a thing. Or you may notice they are stubborn and want to stick around. In this case, when you are done practicing distress tolerance, gently shift your focus to something in your environment. This will ground you in the present moment.

The more you can sit with unpleasant thoughts and feelings without trying to change them or make them go away, the more you will be able to tolerate and accept the distress that is part of roller derby. Practice tolerating distress as you move through your daily life. When you notice you are upset, acknowledge the sensations, emotions, and thoughts, but don't immediately try to change them or make them go away. Coexist with them for a moment or two.

(See page 172 for a distress tolerance activity.)

# MENTAL TOUGHNESS TOOL
## BE STRONG:
## GUIDED MEDITATION FOR
## FINDING YOUR STRENGTHS AND ABILITIES

With eyes closed or gaze softened, imagine you are stepping into a beautiful forest. There is a clear path ahead of you and it seems so inviting you can't help but follow it. You feel completely safe and at ease, relaxed. You walk along the path, noticing all the forest life around you. Plants, trees, flowers, creatures large and small, the smell of the forest, the feeling of air on your skin, the temperature is just right for you, not too hot or too cold, notice the sounds happening around you, you feel relaxed and at peace.

After walking for a while along the forest path, the trees thin out and you come to a clearing. In the clearing you see a small cabin, it feels very welcoming and you want to go up to the door, you walk toward the cabin and open the door. Inside the cabin you see someone who is special to you. It could be someone you know now, knew in the past, or never knew but wanted to. Looking at this person, you can see they want to tell you something important. As you move closer they tell you they want you to know what your strengths and abilities are. You listen closely to what they tell you.

When you are ready, open your eyes and fill in the shield on the next page with words, symbols, or pictures depicting your strengths and abilities. How can you use these strengths and abilities to help you in your roller derby performance?

# MENTAL TOUGHNESS TOOL
## BE BALANCED: TUNE UP YOUR CHAKRAS

What the heck is a chakra? At its heart, the chakra is a "wheel" or vortex-like powerhouse of energy inside of us. The concept of chakra comes from esoteric, medieval-era Indian traditions. Our psychological, spiritual, and emotional self is said to contain energy channels connected by nodes called chakras. In Buddhist and Hindu philosophy, the main seven chakras are thought to be arranged in a column along the spinal cord, from its base to the top of the head. The tantric traditions sought to master, awaken, and energize them through various techniques.

Sometimes chakras become blocked because of stress or emotional or physical problems. If the body's energy system can't flow freely, one may feel mentally and emotionally out of balance. Tuning up the chakras is the process of restoring a harmonious flow of energy across the chakra system. The effect of balanced chakras often translates into a feeling of well-being, relaxation, centeredness, and increased vitality.

The chart on the following page contains emotional qualities that correspond to balanced and unbalanced chakras and affirmations you can make to tune up your chakra system if needed. The symbols for each chakra on page 206 can be decorated in the rainbow of colors noted in each one's description.

| Name | Balance | Imbalance | Tune-Up With These Affirmations |
|---|---|---|---|
| Crown Chakra, Violet | Loving, aware, wise, inspired | Dogmatic, judgmental, angry, cynical | I honor my body as my temple. I am peaceful, whole, and balanced. I am grateful for my healthy, strong body. |
| Third Eye Chakra, Indigo | Imaginative, intuitive, clear thoughts, peace of mind | Lack of focus, obsessive, poor intuition, denial, depression | I am passionate, powerful, and productive. I am guided by my inner wisdom. I am at all times safe, loved, and protected. |
| Throat Chakra, Blue | Clear communicator, diplomatic, advocate for self and others | Bossy, difficulty listening, can't express self, overly talkative | I am calm, confident, and centered. I easily speak my truth. I own my power and feel fully alive. |
| Heart Chakra, Green | Peaceful, compassionate, warm, open | Lack of empathy, narcissistic, hateful, intolerant, jealous | I feel stronger, more alive, and energized each day. I deserve love, health, happiness and success. I love and accept myself just as I am. |
| Solar Plexus Chakra, Yellow | Confident, empowered, in control, good self-image, ambitious | Low self-esteem, perfectionistic, lack of will power, aggression | I give myself permission to fully enjoy everything I do. I am a powerful, radiant, magnificent being. I love myself, I value myself, I trust myself. |
| Sacral Chakra, Orange | Passionate, creative, optimistic, trusting | Overemotional, creative block, guilt | I am beyond capable. I am creative and courageous. I listen to my inner truth. |
| Root Chakra, Red | Centered, happy to be alive, courageous, resolved | Fearful, anxious, ungrounded, power hungry, spacey | I am fully grounded and supported. I have enough, I know enough, I am enough. I nourish my heart, mind, and body. |

# MENTAL TOUGHNESS TIP #77
## Improve Visual Focus

When you improve your visual focusing skills, you can eliminate visual distractions and lock-in your concentration. The exercise below will help you to build this skill.

1. Look at the focusing target of the jammer star below until everything else disappears.
2. Think only about the star.
3. If your mind wanders, gently bring your focus back to the star.
4. Don't actively try to shut out competing thoughts, simply acknowledge them and bring your attention back to the star.

# MENTAL TOUGHNESS TIP #78
## Optimize Your Field Of Awareness

When we are stressed, it narrows the field of our awareness. This is due to our natural stress response in which the body and mind eliminate unnecessary functioning and distractions, channeling our resources to where they are needed most. Our field of vision narrows, our hearing becomes more sensitive, and our thought processes become simplified.

However, if we are too stressed, or hyper-aroused, our focus becomes so narrow that we can't operate on the track. We are in danger of tunnel vision and an inability to see the bigger picture. If we are too relaxed, or hypo-aroused, our focus will be too wide, and we will lack the intensity needed to kick ass. The squiggly line on the figure on the following page shows the optimal area in our field of awareness for an excellent performance, not too narrow or too wide.

Once you can recognize what state you are in, hypo-aroused or hyper-aroused, you can do what your system needs to bring it back to homeostasis. If you are hypo-aroused your system needs to be alerted and engaged. If you are hyper-aroused your system needs to be soothed. It is in the middle, in this window between hypo-arousal and hyper-arousal, where you function at your best. Here you will have the optimal amount of focus, integrating the ideal amount of sensory information around you which will lead to decisive and responsive play.

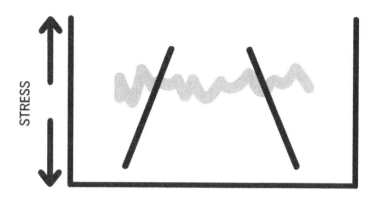

(See page 45 for ways to get into your green zone.)

# MENTAL TOUGHNESS TIP #79
## Stabilize Your Confidence

Confidence comes from several sources, both internal and external:
- A practice environment where it feels safe to make mistakes
- Feeling prepared—physically and mentally
- Seeing others performing a skill
- Trusting your coaches and teammates
- Having the support of family and friends
- Feeling good about one's body
- Feeling healthy
- Noting the development and improvement of your skills

Some sources of confidence are under your control and some aren't. True confidence is based on having control of your perceptions, emotions, and behavior. This type of confidence is very stable, and it takes quite a lot to shake it. Confidence that depends solely on coaches, teammates, or favorable situations is an inconsistent type of self-confidence. Stable confidence comes from within. We can stabilize our confidence by focusing on our perceptions, emotions, and behavior.

**Perceptions.** Focusing on those things that make you feel confident will lead you to believe you can do anything. The biggest source of feeling confident is past accomplishments. If you succeeded at something in the past, you will think you can do it, or something similar, again. Conversely, if you failed at something in the past, you may not believe you can do it in the future. If you need help building your confidence, plan your next steps on skills you now have. Going too big, too soon can make you feel like things are out of reach. Keep the focus on what you can do and build from there.

**Emotions.** Lack of confidence comes from one place: fear. When we allow ourselves to be driven by our fears, we lose control over our ability to achieve our goals.
- Fear about what people will think of you
- Fear of failure
- Fear of success
- Fear of injury

Face these fears head on. Acknowledge the fear, see what it is trying to tell you, but know you don't have to listen to it.

**Behavior.** Our actions build our confidence, but it takes confidence to act. At some point you must break into this cycle using will power. Push yourself and see what you can do! You may be pleasantly surprised. Most people stop when things start getting difficult. Be the one who perseveres. Every time you push yourself just past that place you didn't think you could go, your confidence grows.

*Confidence is all about action.*

# MENTAL TOUGHNESS TOOL
## BE ATTENTIVE: IMPROVE YOUR MEMORY

Memorizing stuff is a great way to exercise your mental muscles and improve your attentional control. For this exercise, get a tray (a baking pan will work) and place 5-10 random items on it. Allow yourself 30 seconds to memorize the items. Cover the tray and write down as many items as you can recall. Then take the cover off and check your accuracy. If you didn't get them all correct, try it again with fewer items. If you got it easily, challenge yourself by adding more items.

Here are some other ways to improve your memory muscles and attentional control:

1. Memorize inspirational writings. Memorize a poem, book passage, or verse of scripture each week.
2. Create a "not to-do list." If you are in the middle of something, resist the urge to go to your e-sources every time you have a question or want to look something up. Allow these impulses time to mellow by writing the thought down on paper. If you still care later, do your research.
3. Watch an old movie. Today we are used to fast cuts and lots of visual and auditory stimulation. The pacing and content of movies used to be much simpler, allowing you time to pay attention to details.

# MENTAL TOUGHNESS TIP FOR TEAMS #80
### Find Unity

In games where there is a lot on the line, tensions can run high. Some teams may find themselves attacking each other when they should be targeting the opposing team. By presenting a divided rather than united front, you have already given the other team an advantage over you. The true definition of a team is a whole greater than the sum of its parts. To accomplish this, it may mean putting your own wants aside. Find unity in your common goal—kicking ass!

Create a ritual to get everyone refocused and on the same page. Below are some ideas to get you started:
- Mid-game cheer
- Pass a high-five down the bench
- Mini crowd-wave on your bench (maybe it will spread around the venue!)

# MENTAL TOUGHNESS TIP #81
## Harness The Power Of Positive Thought
## aka Suppress The White Bear

Our thoughts are the things our mind tells us. Thoughts include the attitudes, beliefs, perceptions, ideas, and images we hold in our head. Our thoughts are everything because they are the summary of all the sensory information our body and mind gathers and synthesizes. They are the way we understand the world and our place in it.

We have around 50,000 thoughts per day and up to 70% of them can be negative. This negativity bias is nature's way of helping us stay aware of potential threats, but if we let this take over, it will decrease our confidence and drive.

In 1863, Fyodor Dostoyevsky noted in his *Winter Notes on Summer Impressions*, "try to pose for yourself this task: to not think of a polar bear, and you will see that cursed thing will come to mind every minute." Daniel Wegner, the noted thought suppression expert, decided to research this concept and found that the more we try not to think of something, the more we think about it later. If we consider the white bear to be like negative thoughts, simply trying not to think negatively just doesn't work and may even make it worse.

Here are some tips from Wegner for suppressing the white bear:
1. Pick an absorbing distractor and focus on that instead. Choose something that is positive and easy to shift your focus to such as a red balloon.
2. Try to postpone the thought. Create a fifteen-minute period each day dedicated to worrying. Then when a

negative thought pops up, you can tell yourself, "I will think of that later."

3. Cut back on multitasking. A 2013 article in *Pharmacy and Therapeutics* discusses how those under increased mental stress show an increase in catastrophic thinking. Multitasking doesn't make you more productive, but it does make you stressed.

4. Exposure. Allow yourself to think about the thing you want to avoid. Then it won't be as likely to come up at other times.

5. Meditation and mindfulness. With the increased mental control that these practices give, you will be able to better avoid or be less affected by unwanted thoughts.

# MENTAL TOUGHNESS TOOL
## BE BALANCED: TREE POSE

Trees provide us with fruit to eat, shade to rest in, paper to write on, branches to climb, and wood for our homes. The longer a tree lives, the more layers it puts on. Trees are connected to the earth and reach for the sky. If their roots aren't deep, they tumble over.

The tree pose energizes, focuses attention, and balances the mind and body. Stand with your feet hip distance apart. Shift your weight onto your left foot. Slowly bend your right knee and draw your right foot up, placing the sole as high as possible on the inner left leg without strain (ankle, shin, or above the knee, just not on the knee). Ground your standing leg down, rooting yourself like a tree to the earth. Press your palms together at heart center. Breathe in and stretch your arms and head up, growing your branches toward the sky. Finding something outside of yourself to focus on will help you stay balanced. Hold for five to eight breaths. Repeat on the other side.

While you are in tree pose, you may choose to consider the following;
1. When am I solid like an oak and when do I waiver like a willow?
2. How am I branching out?
3. In which areas do I need to grow?

Notice being balanced is not a static destination, it requires dynamic movements, some large and some minute to maintain balance.

# MENTAL TOUGHNESS TIP #82
**Find Your Purpose**

You can do anything if you have a good enough reason. Failure to achieve your goals may have more to do with this than anything else. Reassess WHY you want to achieve your goals. Why are your goals important to you? Which of your values are your goals aligned with? Below are some values to consider.

| | |
|---|---|
| Success | Authenticity |
| Determination | Family |
| Health | Fun |
| Belonging | Creativity |
| Challenge | Loyalty |
| Independence | Trustworthiness |
| Wealth | Faith |
| Recognition | Respect |

To help you discover your values, ask yourself the following questions:

*What is my roller derby goal?*
*Why is that important to me?*

You may have to repeatedly ask yourself the second question until you unbury your core values. Linking your goal to a value close to your heart will help you commit to it. If you don't have a reason your goal is important to you, then set a new goal.

Write in your values at the top of the Values Mountain on the following page. Reaching for these values is the reason you do the hard work!

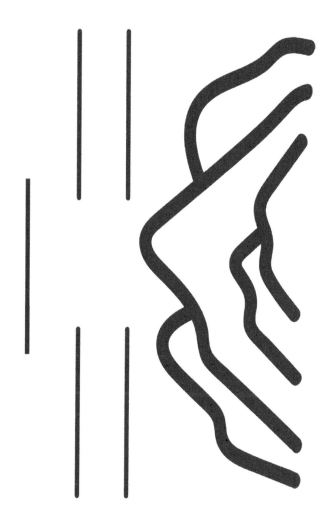

*Adapted with permission from Casey Jackson,
Institute for Individual and Organizational Change.*

# MENTAL TOUGHNESS TIP #83
## Focus On What You Can Control

Focus on what you can control to feel empowered. Use the three concentric circles on the following page to write or draw the things that are under your control, under your influence, and outside of your control. Notice the area for what you can control is the smallest one. When you let go of attempts to control those things that are outside of your control you will experience a decrease in frustration, anger, and anxiety. This will allow you more energy to focus on those things you can control or influence.

Many things are outside of your control such as forces of nature and other people's choices, beliefs, and actions:
- Opponent mouthing off to you
- The weather

Sometimes you can influence situations and outcomes:
- Getting enough sleep
- Getting injured

Many people believe their thoughts and reactions are not under their control, but everything we say, do, or think can be controlled:
- Mouthing off to a referee
- Throwing your water bottle when upset

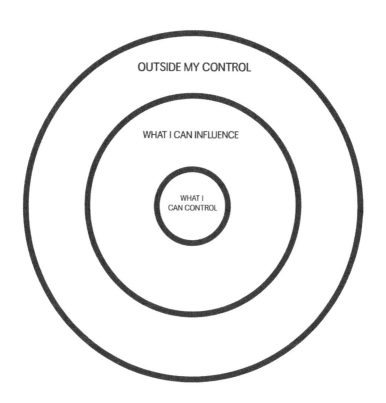

# MENTAL TOUGHNESS TIP #84
## Learn To Reset And Let Go
### (every jam is a new jam)

Learning to let go of a game moment that didn't go your way allows you to always have a fresh start. Otherwise the anger, frustration, self-doubt, or fear will stay with you and inhibit your ability to play your best. Take the time in between jams to reset.

1. Inhale through your nose while making your hand into a fist. Imagine yourself holding the thing that you want to let go.
2. Exhale out your mouth and as you do, open your hand and silently say, "Let it go." Imagine all your frustrations, anger, or worries flying out of your hand and far away from you. Make your exhalation long and loud.

With practice, you will be able to live in the moment, not holding onto what just happened like heavy baggage. You will be light, fresh, and ready for what happens next.

# MENTAL TOUGHNESS TOOL FOR FRESH MEAT TIP #85
## Don't Be Sorry (for learning)

Skaters at all levels are learning in roller derby and this means mistakes are going to be made in the process. Constantly apologizing for every little "oops" moment is unnecessary. There can be an expectation from all that unintentional forearms are going to be flying.

"Sorry" is a golden word that shouldn't be overused. Instead you can say, "Let me try that again," or "I can do better." Save the apologies for when they are heartfelt and warranted like if you accidentally break your teammate's nose.

# MENTAL TOUGHNESS TIP #86
## Cool Off Before Confronting Teammates

Allow yourself and others time to cool off before hashing out beefs.

1. Cool off. Allow others involved time to cool off too (this happens at a different pace for everyone). This may mean taking slow, deep breaths, skating some laps, sitting out of some drills, or leaving practice entirely and taking the issue back up another day. Allowing yourself time to cool off before dealing with the issue will help you avoid reacting from an emotional, heated state. This is being responsible.
2. Talk to those involved directly. Do this outside of practice time or after practice where others can't hear you. Avoid talking to others who are not involved in the problem as this makes the problem (and negativity) spread. You may want to vent to a teammate about what happened, and this can help you cope with the emotions, but you must balance this with doing something about your problem.
3. Know when to involve leadership. If the problem isn't resolved by talking to those involved, take the issue to your coaches, captain, grievance committee, or other leadership so they can help you.

If the situation involves something egregious such as a serious safety concern, major theft, or sexual harassment, do not try to solve it yourself. Immediately involve your leadership.

## Have A Fire Drill

You don't want to figure out how to respond to a fire when it is raging. The same is true for handling an inner firestorm. Practice cooling off when you are cool, and your mind and body will know what to do when you are heated.

## My Cool Off Plan

Where I will go:

_____

_____

What I will do (Positive self-talk, calming or releasing activities):

_____

_____

*(For specific steps to take to resolve conflicts see page 102.)*

# MENTAL TOUGHNESS TOOL
## BE PRESENT: LISTEN

One way to improve your focus is to practice attentive listening. Being attentive isn't just useful for sports, it is also an essential interpersonal skill. The ability to be fully present with family, friends, or teammates builds your intimacy and trust. It shows that person that they are valuable to you. Trying to focus all your energy on someone else also strengthens your concentration muscles making it a win-win. The next time you're talking with someone special, set aside any distractions and listen as attentively as possible:

- Don't interrupt
- *Look* like you're listening with body language that shows you are interested in receiving their message
- Make eye contact
- Don't just *hear* the words the person is saying, attempt to *understand*
- Recap what the other person says to show you are paying attention
- Use connecting words such as "Ah I see," "Yes," and "Ok" to stay engaged

# MENTAL TOUGHNESS TOOL FOR TEAMS
## BE SUPPORTIVE: GOT YOUR BACK

This simple, yet powerful activity allows skaters to experience the undying support of their teammates.

1. Partner up and sit back to back.
2. Spend one silent minute like this, feeling the warmth and unwavering solidity of your teammate's back against yours.
3. Afterwards, discuss what the experience was like. What thoughts and emotions did this bring up?

*I got your back!*

# MENTAL TOUGHNESS TIP #87
## Acknowledge Your Supports

There are many people supporting you on your roller derby journey. You have teammates, family, friends, coaches and more who are there for you.

Fill in the circles on the next page with the names (or roles if you don't know their name) of all the people who support you. The ones who are closer to you will be in the innermost circles and those who aren't as close will be further out. Don't forget to add community members such as the person who makes your coffee, massages your sore muscles, tapes your shoulder, puts the name/number on the back of your jersey, and fixes your skates.

Realizing you have so many people who support you will give you the confidence to achieve anything you want to!

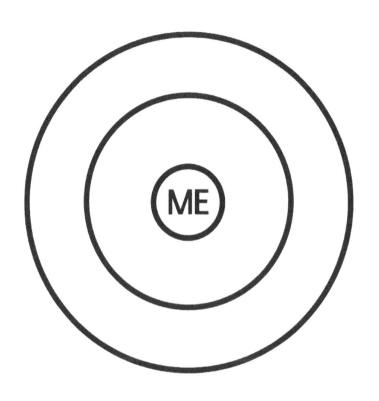

# MENTAL TOUGHNESS TIP #88
## Welcome Your Emotions

Biologically, our feelings and emotions are part of our feedback system. They are designed to help us survive. Richard Miller, who created the iRest Program, calls our emotions *messengers* because they give us useful information about the actions we need to take to get what we need. If you avoid or react to your feelings and emotions, you can't accurately respond to your inner and outer world.

If you welcome every feeling and emotion that comes your way as a messenger, you can use the information they deliver to achieve your full potential. Below is a guided meditation to help you do this (adapted with permission from the book, T*he iRest Program for Healing PTSD).*

### Proactively Engaging Feelings and Emotions

With your eyes open or closed, take a few moments to experience the feeling and mood of your body. Locate a feeling or emotion that's present. Sense where and how you experience this feeling or emotion in your body. Now imagine this feeling or emotion walking in through a door or stepping into a meadow. Go with the first image that appears in your imagination.
What does your feeling or emotion look like? What is its shape, form, color, size? Is it formless, or does it take the shape of a mineral, rock, plant, animal or person? If it is a human being, how old is it, how is it dressed? Take a few moments and simply welcome, with your imagination, the shape and form your feeling or emotion takes.

Now imagine this feeling or emotion standing or sitting in a chair at a comfortable distance in front of you. You're going to ask your feeling or emotion three questions. First, you'll ask it your question. Then you'll imagine yourself as the feeling or emotion speaking the answer back to you.

Now face your feeling or emotion and ask it, *What do you want?* Now imagine you are your feeling or emotion speaking the answer. Listen to what it has to say.

Next ask it, *What do you need?* Now imagine you are your feeling or emotion speaking the answer. Listen to what it has to say.

Finally ask it, *What action are you asking me to take?* Now imagine you are your feeling or emotion speaking the answer. Listen to what it has to say.

Take a few moments to reflect on what you've experienced in your mind and body. Any actions you've discovered that you need to take become intentions. When you set an intention, be sure to follow through with it in your daily life. Following through with your actions and intentions builds confidence.

# MENTAL TOUGHNESS TIP #89
## Set S.M.A.R.T. Goals

Goals need to be clear for us to know we are making (or not making) progress. The acronym, S.M.A.R.T. stands for specific, measurable, action-oriented, realistic, and time-limited.

**Specific:** Goals should be clear, not vague or general. Instead of saying, I want to be a stronger jammer" try "I want to be able to get through the pack on my own, without assistance."

**Measurable:** There should be a way to measure your success. Include elements that can be measured such as the number of penalties, number of laps, number of points, number of assists, etc.

**Action-oriented:** Your goal should be about things you want to do, not things you don't want to do. Use the "rock rule." If a rock can do it, it isn't a good goal. For example, the goal "I'm not going to swear today" isn't the greatest goal because a rock can do that. Try making the goal into something that requires you to act such as, "I will say 'thank you' when someone helps me."

**Realistic:** Choose a goal that is something you are both willing and able to do. Goals should be difficult enough to challenge you, but realistic enough to be achievable. Based on how far you've come, where do you think you can go?

**Time-limited:** Establish a deadline for accomplishing your goal. Time frames give you a sense of urgency that can be motivating. A good guideline is to set goals you can achieve within three to six months.

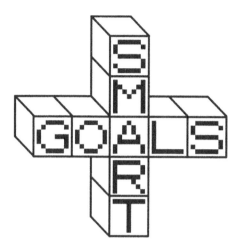

You can make your goals even S.M.A.R.T.E.R. by evaluating and re-evaluating them on a regular basis. Write your goal down and put it somewhere you can see it every day.

If you achieve your goal ahead of schedule, then set a new one. If you haven't made any progress at all, look at how the goal may need to be adjusted.

Specific
Measurable
Action-oriented
Realistic
Time-limited
Evaluate
Re-evaluate

# MENTAL TOUGHNESS TOOL
## BE INSPIRED: LIVE BY YOUR MOTTO

Who we are is ultimately defined by the actions we take. But it can be difficult to know what direction to go in without a moral compass as a guide. When you are struggling for direction, having a good life motto can provide light in the darkness.

Use the scroll on the next page to write down your own life motto. A good one can inspire us to act, overcome obstacles, and stay determined. It motivates us to be our best self during the toughest times. Here are some famous ones for inspiration:

"Just keep swimming."
-Dory, *Finding Nemo*

"Get busy living or get busy dying."
-Stephen King, *Shawshank Redemption*

"Lead without followers, live from within."
-Dave Ursillo, *Lead*

"Be like the sun and you shall warm the earth."
-Angela Artimus, *Powered by Intuition*

"Let it be."
-Paul McCartney

# MENTAL TOUGHNESS TIP #90
## Prevent Focus Failure

There are three types of focus failure:
1. Focus is too wide. When we focus on too many things at once our performance suffers. Intensify your focus to the vital elements of the game and your performance will improve. Non-essential things that could take your focus are crowd noise, announcers, and trash talk by an opposing skater.
2. Focusing on the wrong thing. An example of this is a skater getting emotionally caught up in a call by a referee that is perceived as undeserved. If the skater continues to focus on their feeling of injustice it will prevent them from playing their best.
3. Focus too narrow or unable to shift rapidly enough. This is commonly seen in roller derby when a team is overly focused on assisting and totally misses the opposing jammer skating through the pack. A skater needs to be able to shift fast enough between the vital aspects of the game situation or to widen their focus to take more in.

Coaches, teammates, and others can cause another kind of focusing problem called *inattentional blindness*. This happens when your coach or teammates tell you a specific game element to focus on such as watching out for a certain skater or avoiding a certain penalty. The problem with this is it is based on what just happened rather than what is currently happening. A skater may become too focused on what they were told, leading to unresponsiveness, or "blindness," to the current game situation.

A last type of focusing issue is called *failure focus*. This happens when coaches, friends, teammates, and others repeatedly ask questions or make comments such as, "Why did you do that?" or "You really screwed that up" when a skater makes a mistake or doesn't live up to their expectations. These types of questions or comments can cause a skater to become overly focused on what they did wrong instead of what they need to do to achieve excellence. Focus on the right things at the right time and watch your game grow!

# MENTAL TOUGHNESS TIP #91
## Improve Auditory Focus

Focus in sports is multisensory, meaning we use many different senses when focusing. Our vision is used to track the opposing jammer. We use our hearing to listen for the jam start whistle. Our sense of touch is used to set up a strong defense with our teammates. We may even use our sense of taste and smell. Our focus must be put into those elements that are essential to the moment. By improving your auditory focus, you will be able to "tune out" any unnecessary or distracting sounds during a game and be alert only those sounds necessary to your performance. Try this exercise to improve your auditory focus:

Sit quietly with your eyes closed. Bring your attention to the sound of your breath as it moves in and out through your nose. Take several breaths in this way. Now bring your attention to the sounds occurring around you. Try to pick out one individual sound and focus on it completely, ignoring all the others. Now hear all the sounds around you at once. Let them blend together without trying to differentiate them. Now pick another single sound and bring it to the forefront of your awareness, again tuning out all the other sounds. Now hear all the sounds simultaneously. Go back and forth like this several times, first listening to just one sound, and then listening to all the sounds at once.

## MENTAL TOUGHNESS TOOL
### BE CALM: PROGRESSIVE MUSCLE RELAXATION

Progressive Muscle Relaxation is based on three assumptions:
a) It is possible to learn the difference between tension and relaxation.
b) Tension and relaxation are mutually exclusive.
c) Relaxation of the body through decreased muscle tension will in turn decrease mental tension.

In each step you'll first tense a muscle group, release it halfway, and then relax it completely. Pay close attention to how it feels to be relaxed as opposed to tense. For each muscle group, you can perform each exercise twice before progressing to the next muscle group. As you gain skill, you can omit the tension phase and focus just on relaxation.

1. Get in a comfortable position with limbs uncrossed. Take a deep breath, let it out slowly, as you exhale focus on the spreading relaxation.
2. Make a tight fist with each hand. Notice the uncomfortable tension in your hands and fingers. Hold that tension, then let go halfway and hold. Exhale and let your hands relax completely. Notice how the tension and discomfort drain from your hands, replaced by comfort and relaxation. Focus on the contrast between the tension you felt and the relaxation you now feel. Concentrate on relaxing your hands completely.
3. Tense your upper arms tightly and focus on the tension. Let the tension out halfway and hold, focusing on the tension. Exhaling, relax your upper arms completely, focusing on the developing relaxation.

4. Curl your toes as tight as you can and hold. Relax the toes halfway. Exhaling, relax your toes completely and focus on the spreading relaxation.

5. Point your toes away from you and tense your feet and calves. Hold the tension hard, then let it out halfway. Exhaling, relax your feet and calves completely.

6. Extend your legs and tense your thigh muscles. Hold the tension, let it out halfway and hold. Exhaling, relax your thighs completely. Concentrate on the sensation of relaxation in your feet, calves, and thighs.

7. Tense your stomach muscles as tight as you can, concentrating on the tension. Let the tension out halfway and hold. Exhaling, relax your stomach muscles completely. Focus on the spreading relaxation until your stomach muscles are completely relaxed.

8. Tighten your chest and shoulder muscles and hold. Let go halfway and hold. Exhaling, relax the muscles and concentrate on the deepening relaxation until your muscles are completely loose and relaxed. Your hands, arms, toes, feet, calves, thighs, stomach, chest, shoulders completely relaxed.

9. Tense your back muscles and hold. Let the tension out halfway, hold the reduced tension, and focus on it. Exhaling, relax your back muscles completely, focusing on the relaxation spreading over the entire area.

10. Keeping your torso, arms, and legs relaxed, tense your neck muscles. Hold. Release the tension halfway and hold. Exhaling, relax your neck completely. Allow your head to rest comfortably while you focus on the relaxation developing in your neck muscles.

11. Clench your teeth and feel the tension in the muscles of your jaw. Let the tension out halfway and hold. Exhaling, relax the jaw muscles. Let your mouth and facial muscles relax completely.

12. Wrinkle your forehead and scalp as tightly as you can and hold. Release halfway and hold. Exhaling, relax your scalp and forehead completely, focusing on the feeling of relaxation and contrasting it with the earlier tension. Concentrate on relaxing all the muscles of your body. Your hands, arms, toes, feet, calves, thighs, stomach, chest, shoulders, back, neck, jaw, forehead and scalp completely relaxed.

13. (Cue-controlled relaxation) Think of a word that means relaxation to you. It could be *calm, still, peace*, or simply *relax*. Take a deep breath in, filling the belly, ribs and chest. Hold the breath in the back of your throat, then exhale slowly while thinking your relaxation cue word. Repeat this several times, inhaling and exhaling, thinking your relaxation cue word, each time striving to deepen your state of relaxation.

# MENTAL TOUGHNESS TIP #92
**Find Your Fight Song**

Musical activities have been present in every known culture on earth extending back 250,000 years or more. Music has been shown to fulfill three important functions for mental toughness: it helps us relate to others, it regulates our arousal and mood, and it allows us to achieve self-awareness.

Music:
- Calms us down or relaxes us
- Comforts us when we are sad
- Gives us a container for our anger or frustration
- Acts as an escape from our worries and stress
- Makes us feel energized and powerful
- Allows us to get to know ourselves better
- Enables us to feel connected to others
- Lets others know what we think
- Is a means of self-expression
- Puts us in a good mood
- Can help us dream
- Allows us to experiment with our identity

Listening to the right song can turn on your performance. Dr. Costas Karageorghis, professor of sport and exercise psychology at Brunel University London, says music is "a type of legal performance-enhancing drug." While you can't always listen to your choice of music during games, you can choose what you listen to while warming up. Pick a song that puts you in the right state of mind for the game—confident, energized, focused, calm, and alert—ready to kick ass.

# MENTAL TOUGHNESS TIP FOR TEAMS #93
## Give The Other Team Their Win

There are many reasons, such as those below, that a team may give for losing a game:
- Skating short
- Missing key players
- Being treated unfairly by the refs
- Slippery skating surface
- Skaters had the flu
- Lots of new skaters
- Temperature too hot
- Half the team playing injured

Allow the winning team to enjoy their sweet taste of victory without souring it with your excuses. Simply tell the other team, "Great game!" and "Congratulations!" Keep the laundry list of reasons for your loss to your team. Next time mitigate those factors and bring your best game.

# MENTAL TOUGHNESS TIP #94
## Welcome Opposites Of Thought

Every thought you have impacts your body. Think the words, *I'm capable.* Now think, *I can't do it, I suck.* Just by reading these opposites of thought, your thyroid, spleen, pancreas, and adrenal glands are responding to your thoughts. They are sending out chemicals that influence your immune system, cardiovascular system, respiratory system, and digestive system.

Most spend a lot of time avoiding the negative thought in a pair of opposites. But one half can't exist without the other half. When we push away the thought of ineptitude, we prevent ourselves from feeling capable. Welcoming the opposites of life—capable and powerless, sad and happy, fear and safety will allow us to find wholeness and freedom.

Due to our brain's negativity bias, we perceive the negative half of thoughts easier. To move to the positive aspect of a thought more readily, it may help to have a middle step that is neither a negative nor positive extreme.

**Negative thought:** *I can't do it, I'm powerless*
**Middle step:** *I can do some part of this*
**Positive thought:** *I'm capable*

1. When you encounter the negative opposite of a thought
    a) Stay calm
    b) Embrace the thought
    c) See what it wants

2. Know that a thought is just something your mind is telling you. It is not necessarily the truth.

3. Thoughts have a lifecycle and are born to die. Just like any living thing, thoughts go through a birth, growth, period of stability, decay, and a death. Wait long enough and the thought will change.

# MENTAL TOUGHNESS TIP #95
## Fake It 'Til You Make It

Confidence is the belief that you can succeed. It is solidly built on your achievements. Confidence builds when you take action and try things you find hard, when you go outside your comfort zone. Confidence is all about action, and action gets you results.

When others perceive you as confident, they will believe in your ability to get the job done. This will, in turn, help *you* to believe in your ability to meet challenges. When you do, and accomplish something amazing, this creates true confidence. This means the strategy, "fake it 'til you make it" is a good way to start building confidence!

Here are some ways to act big and bold and appear more confident to others:

**Hold your head up.** The old saying, "Keep your chin up," referred to telling someone not to give up. Someone who has their head up is still in the game.

**Make eye contact.** Without being creepy, think of interactions as a staring contest that you are going to win.

**Big gestures.** There is an idea that the bigger you are, the more of a leader you are. Taking up more space with your body makes you appear bigger. Claim your territory.

**Ground yourself before speaking.** Solidly plant both of your feet on the surface you're standing on. This will ensure you have even footing and a stable foundation.

**Stand tall.** Make your spine as long as possible, keep your shoulders back, and reach the crown of your head toward the sky. Channel the posture of a superhero.

**Try fronting.** This means pointing your toes and torso toward the person you are talking to. It will make you look focused, put together, and charismatic.

**Speak from the belly.** Your core is your place of confidence. Deliver your words from this place and they will carry weight.

**Have an authoritative tone.** When answering questions, leave out the doubting, questioning inflection. Answer with a firm tone that lets people know your certainty.

**Smile.** A genuine smile can put others at ease and invoke trust, making them more receptive to you.

The amazing part is, if you begin to do these things, you will *become* more confident. Your brain will pick up on what your body is doing, and you won't have to fake it any longer. Need another reason for building confidence? Confidence is contagious, so the more confident you are, the more confident your whole team will be.

# MENTAL TOUGHNESS TOOL
## BE MINDFUL: MINDFULNESS QUIZ

Come back and take this Mindfulness Attention Awareness Scale (MAAS) every now and then to see if your skills need a tune-up.

Instructions: Below is a collection of statements about your everyday experience. Using the 1-6 scale below, please indicate how frequently or infrequently you currently have each experience. Please answer according to what really reflects your experience rather than what you think your experience should be. Please treat each item separately from every other item.

| 1 | 2 | 3 | 4 | 5 | 6 |
|---|---|---|---|---|---|
| Always | Frequently | Somewhat frequently | Somewhat infrequently | Infrequently | Never |

I could be experiencing some emotion and not be conscious of it until somewhat later.
1    2    3    4    5    6

I break or spill things because of carelessness, not paying attention, or thinking of something else.
1    2    3    4    5    6

I find it difficult to stay focused on what's happening in the present.
1    2    3    4    5    6

I tend to walk quickly to get where I'm going without paying attention to what I experience along the way.
    1         2         3         4         5         6

I tend not to notice feelings of physical tension or discomfort until they really grab my attention.
    1         2         3         4         5         6

I forget a person's name almost as soon as I've been told it for the first time.
    1         2         3         4         5         6

It seems I am "running on automatic" without much awareness of what I'm doing.
    1         2         3         4         5         6

I rush through activities without being really attentive to them.
    1         2         3         4         5         6

I get so focused on the goal I want to achieve that I lose touch with what I'm doing right now to get there.
    1         2         3         4         5         6

I do jobs or tasks automatically, without being aware of what I'm doing.
    1         2         3         4         5         6

I find myself listening to someone with one ear, doing something else at the same time.
    1        2        3        4        5        6

I go places on "automatic pilot" and then wonder why I went there.
    1        2        3        4        5        6

I find myself preoccupied with the future or the past.
    1        2        3        4        5        6

I find myself doing things without paying attention.
    1        2        3        4        5        6

I snack without being aware that I'm eating.
    1        2        3        4        5        6

Scoring: To score the MAAS scale, simply add your score for the 15 items. Scores will range from 15 to 90. Higher scores reflect higher levels of mindfulness.

# MENTAL TOUGHNESS TIP #96
## Focus On Solutions

*Expectancy Theory* states that which we focus on expands. It seems like such a simple idea, to just focus on what we want to have more of in life. However, it is way easier for individuals to focus on problems than solutions.

It is necessary to turn this around because it affects an athlete's confidence. If a person is focused on the things they can do well, they will feel confident. If they are focused on shortcomings, their confidence will tank. A confident athlete is much more coachable and makes improvements faster because they don't need internal or external convincing that they can do things. The next time you notice you are focusing on something you can't do, immediately ask yourself,

*What is one thing I can do differently that could make this better?*

Let's practice this right now. Think of the biggest problem you currently have with your performance. What is one thing you could do to make it better? Your solution does not have to solve the problem completely, only make an improvement. By using this strategy, you will turn every problem-focused thought into solution-focused thinking. Start focusing on what you can do, not what you can't do, and watch your confidence and your success grow.

*Most people focus on problems,*
*mentally tough people focus on solutions.*

# MENTAL TOUGHNESS TIP #97
## Recognize Indirect Emotions

A direct emotion is one that is appropriately related to a situation. You may feel disappointed because you weren't selected to the travel team. This emotion is directly related to the event. If you work hard for something and wanted it badly, it will feel like a letdown when it doesn't happen.

An indirect emotion comes in response to thoughts in our minds, not the reality that is happening. Let's go back to the skater in the travel team example. They initially felt sad that they weren't selected, but then became angry. The anger came in response to the thoughts in their mind, not the current situation. The sadness brought up beliefs the skater had about their self and their world such as, *Nothing ever goes my way,* or *I wasn't treated fairly*. These thoughts brought on feelings of anger and resentment. Sadness was the direct emotion, it was related to the situation. Anger was the indirect emotion, it was associated to the situation through the skater's thoughts and memories. Something in this situation reminded them of their past. It doesn't make sense to let an emotion that is not directly related to a situation get in the way of our best performance.

Sometimes indirect, or secondary, emotions serve the purpose of helping us to avoid feeling bad. Emotions such as sadness, doubt, and fear can be experienced as weak or vulnerable feelings. Emotions such as anger can be experienced as strong or powerful, feelings which can be easier to deal with or protect us by keeping others away. In time, these responses may become unconsciously automatic.

Anytime there is a danger of feeling bad, we will cover up our true emotions with a more comfortable secondary one.

With self-awareness, you will be able to recognize if you are responding to an emotion that is directly related and relevant to the reality at hand, or indirectly related and triggered by your thoughts. This will make managing your emotional responses easier.

# MENTAL TOUGHNESS TIP #98
## Commit To Your Values

It is vital to understand the difference between motivation and commitment. Motivation is wanting or desiring something, such as, "I really want to make the roster for the next game." Commitment is taking the actions that will take you in the direction of your goals as in, "I am going to practice tonight so that I make the roster for the next game."

*Motivation is nice. Commitment is necessary.*

The D.A.R.N. C.A.T. acronym is helpful in remembering the importance of commitment.
 You must have a
 **D**esire to achieve your goals, an
 **A**bility to achieve your goals, a
 **R**eason to achieve your goals, and a
 **N**eed to achieve your goals to
 **C**ommit to
 **A**ction and
 **T**ake the steps to get there!

Having a reason to achieve your goals is necessary for commitment. Why are your goals important to you? Excitement? Notoriety? Fitness? Friendships? These reasons are your values. Are you ready to commit to your values? This means accepting roller derby as it is, the good, the bad, and the ugly. Committing to your values also means you may have to face fears or take other actions that seem like the opposite of what your automatic urge is.

For example, if you value what's best for your team, then you may have to hand the jammer pantie to someone else when you are feeling tired. You may have to do this even if it is the last jam of the game and you really, really, really love the glory of skating in the last jam of a game.

Mental toughness is a lifelong journey of self-awareness, acceptance of the ongoing difficulties that are part of life, and a commitment to those actions that are most meaningful to you, on and off the track. Accept uncomfortable thoughts and emotions as a normal part of the human experience. Commit to the consistent use of the actions necessary to stay aligned with your values. This will help you achieve your roller derby goals.

---

### Commitment To Values Form

I commit to taking the actions necessary to stay true to my chosen values. I accept that I may not always be feeling or thinking in a way that feels good, but I know I can still focus my attention on what is needed to get the job done.

X_____

# MENTAL TOUGHNESS TIP #99
## Take A Yogic Power Nap

Use the methods of Yoga Nidra practice to achieve complete mental, emotional, and physical relaxation. Yoga Nidra, or "the sleep of the yogis," will take you to a place between sleep and wake where the conscious and the unconscious minds merge. During this psychological rest and rejuvenation, the body can repair muscular, emotional, and mental tensions.

Developing the ability to relax the mind and calm the body helps you control your energy levels and channel your focus. An athlete needs to have an awareness of when their body has had enough or when it needs rest. Yoga Nidra develops this awareness. The key to peak performance is rest. The body needs to run on rest, just as it runs on fuel. If your body can't fully recover, it does not benefit effectively from training or can suffer from overuse injuries.

In the practice of Yoga Nidra, the awareness is rotated between different areas of the body. Follow this script for a short Yoga Nidra power nap.

Lie down on your back. You can make yourself as comfortable as possible with blankets and pillows. Take a few slow, deep breaths, inhaling and exhaling through the nose. Keep your mind alert and tuned in to your breath as this anchors you in the present moment.
Starting with the right pinky toe, move your awareness through each toe one at a time, to the top of the foot, sole of the foot.
Bring your awareness to the inner ankle, outer ankle, lower shin, upper shin, calf, back of the knee, kneecap,

quadricep, lower hamstring, upper hamstring, right glute, left glute, then down the left leg spending time on each area.

Bring your awareness to the lower abdomen, upper abdomen, left side of the chest, middle of the chest, right side of the chest.

Bring your awareness into the right shoulder, right bicep, right tricep, right elbow, forearm, wrist, palm, back of the hand, each finger one at a time, and the thumb.

Bring your awareness into the left shoulder, left bicep, left triceps, left elbow, forearm, wrist, palm, back of the hand, each finger one at a time, and the thumb.

Bring your focus to the throat, back of the neck, jaw, chin, lips, tongue, cheeks, nose, eyes, eyelids, eyebrows, forehead, scalp, crown of the head.

Relax every part, letting go of all tension, feeling your body melt.

Imagine your body is as light as a fluffy, white cloud floating in the sky. Then, visualize your body as heavy as a boulder grounded in the earth. Stay here enjoying the sensations for as long as you want.

Try to spend at least twenty minutes practicing Yoga Nidra on a regular basis. With time, you can build up to longer practices. It can be challenging to stay awake and alert, but the benefits are worth it. A 2009 article in the *Indian Journal of Traditional Medicine* stated there are changes in the brain's alpha waves with even a short Yoga Nidra practice. Alpha waves are the brain waves of being in the here and now. They help with mental coordination, calmness, alertness, and integrating learning between the mind and the body, which are all great for roller derby.

# MENTAL TOUGHNESS TOOL
## BE CONFIDENT: PLANK POSE

Because our mind and body are connected, when we think defeating thoughts it will be reflected in defeated body language. We may hang our head and take short, half-hearted "Charlie Brown" steps. When we are thinking confidently, we hold our head up and take long, self-assured strides. The flip side to the mind-body connection is when we act with confidence, it is reflected in thinking confident thoughts. It is not always easy to control our thoughts, but we can work to have control over our body.

One of the ways yoga boosts confidence is by strengthening the core. A strong core is vital to the physical aspects of playing roller derby. And being strong, stable, and balanced gives you the confidence you need to get out there and kick ass. A solid core also gives confidence beyond that. When you feel strong on the inside, you can start to trust your body's inner wisdom and you stop second guessing yourself. Your inner strength becomes translated into outer strength that you can direct into personal power on and off the track. A strong core equals a confident you!

Come to all fours with shoulders over wrists and hips over knees. Fingers are pointed straight ahead and spread wide. Press your palms down and straighten one leg back, your foot is on the earth with toes curled under. Do the same with the other leg. Lift your legs, hips, belly and head until your whole body is straight like a board. Gaze is slightly forward, keeping the length in the back of the neck. Press out through your heels and the crown of your head. Hold for two to five breaths (or longer!).

(A modified version of this pose, the half-plank, can be done with knees on the ground.)

# MENTAL TOUGHNESS TOOL
## BE FOCUSED:
## SCANNING AND RECOGNITION

**Level I:** Look at the Concentration Grid on the following page. Time yourself touching the boxes that contain ten consecutive numbers (1-9, 10-19, 20-29, etc.). You can also do even numbers, multiples of 3, and so on to mix it up. Try to do this as quickly as possible. Completing this task improves your visual focus. It involves scanning and recognizing the essential information while ignoring the non-essential information.

**Level II:** Add some distractions such as loud music or somebody talking to you.

**Level III:** In addition to distractions, simulate game nerves by doing ten jumping jacks before you try the activity. This will increase your heart rate which is one of the physiological signs of anxiety.

| 84 | 27 | 51 | 78 | 59 | 52 | 13 | 85 | 61 | 55 |
|----|----|----|----|----|----|----|----|----|----|
| 28 | 60 | 92 | 4 | 97 | 90 | 31 | 57 | 29 | 33 |
| 32 | 96 | 65 | 39 | 80 | 77 | 49 | 86 | 18 | 70 |
| 76 | 87 | 71 | 95 | 98 | 81 | 1 | 46 | 88 | 100 |
| 48 | 82 | 89 | 47 | 35 | 17 | 10 | 42 | 62 | 34 |
| 44 | 67 | 93 | 11 | 7 | 43 | 72 | 94 | 69 | 56 |
| 53 | 79 | 5 | 22 | 54 | 74 | 58 | 14 | 91 | 2 |
| 6 | 68 | 99 | 75 | 26 | 15 | 41 | 66 | 20 | 40 |
| 50 | 9 | 64 | 8 | 38 | 30 | 36 | 45 | 83 | 24 |
| 3 | 73 | 21 | 23 | 16 | 37 | 25 | 19 | 12 | 63 |

# MENTAL TOUGHNESS TIP #100
## Use Imagery For Self-Awareness

Sports psychologists, Robin S. Vealey and Christy A. Greenleaf, developed visualization scripts like the following to increase an athlete's sense of self-awareness.

### Self-awareness Exercise 1

Think back and choose a past roller derby performance in which you performed very well. Use all your senses—hearing, touch, smell, sight, and taste—to recreate that situation in your mind. See yourself as you were succeeding, hear the sounds involved, feel your body as you performed the movements, and re-experience the positive emotions. Try to pick out the elements that made you perform so well (intense focus, feelings of confidence, optimal energy levels). After identifying these elements, try to determine why they were present in this situation. Think about the things you did in preparation for this event. What are some things that may have caused this great performance? Repeat this exercise imagining a situation in which you performed very poorly. Make sure you are very relaxed before trying this because your mind will subconsciously resist your imagery attempts to recreate unpleasant thoughts, images, and feelings. Attempt to become more self-aware of how you reacted to different stimuli (coaches, opponents, officials, fear of failure, needing approval from others) and how these thoughts and feelings may have interfered with your performance.

## Self-awareness Exercise 2

Think back to a roller derby situation in which you experienced a great deal of anxiety. Recreate that situation in your head, seeing and hearing yourself. Especially recreate the feeling of anxiety, feeling the physical responses of your body and recalling the thoughts going through your mind that may have caused the anxiety.

Now attempt to let go of the anxiety and relax your body. Breathe slowly and deeply and focus on relaxing your body as you exhale. Imagine all the tension being pulled into your lungs and exhaled from your body. Continue breathing slowly and exhaling tension until you are deeply relaxed. Now repeat this exercise imagining a situation in which you experienced a great deal of anger, frustration, or other emotion you are working with. Then relax yourself using the breathing technique above.

## Self-awareness Exercise 3

The purpose of this exercise is to help you become more aware of the things that happen during competition that bother you when you perform. Think about the times when your performance suddenly went from good to bad. Recreate several of these experiences in your mind. Try to pinpoint the specific factors that negatively influenced your performance (coaches, teammates, opponents' remarks, officials, couldn't let go of a mistake, opponents started to play much better). After becoming aware of the factors that negatively affected your performance, take several minutes to recreate the situations. Develop appropriate strategies to deal with the negative factors. Imagine the situations again, but this time see yourself using your strategies to keep the negative factors from interfering with your performance. Reinforce yourself by feeling proud that you were able to control the negative factors and perform well.

# MENTAL TOUGHNESS TOOL
## BE CALM: WARMING BODY SCAN

Take a comfortable seat. Let your senses open to the environment around you, feeling the sensation of air touching your skin. Bring your attention to your breath. Noting the sensation of your breath, not trying to change it or control it in any way. Feeling your belly gently expand and release with every inhalation and exhalation.

Begin your body scan by bringing your attention to your forehead. Imagine there is a warm light glowing at the center between your eyebrows. Let that warm light dissolve any tension you may be feeling in your forehead.

Now, let that light travel to your jaw. Separate your teeth and release your tongue from the top of your mouth. Move your jaw from side to side, relaxing it. Move the light down to your neck and tops of your shoulders. Allow your shoulders to release away from your ears, as if they are dissolving down into the earth. The light now travels to your abdomen. Feel the cool air coming in and filling your abdomen and leaving your body as warm air.

Spend a minute feeling this cool and warm air.

Feel the warm light travel down your legs to your feet. Let your toes relax. You can wiggle them to make sure. The light now travels to each toe, one at a time, and then rests at the arches of your feet.

Now that this warm light has traveled down your body, let it surround you. This warm, white light extends around you, radiating around you in every direction. Spend some time here, in this warm, glowing light. You are safe. You are relaxed.

# MENTAL TOUGHNESS TIP #101
## Create Change

In the early 1980s, James Prochaska and Carlo DiClemente created a model to explain the process of change. Setting out to achieve your roller derby goal is setting out to make a change. Knowing that there are stages people go through when undertaking a change can clarify where you're at in this process and how to move yourself forward. There are five stages of change: precontemplation, contemplation, preparation, action, and maintenance.

1. Precontemplation (not ready). If you are at this stage, you are not ready to do anything differently than you are doing right now. You may not be ready because you don't believe you can do it or have had bad experiences trying to achieve goals in the past. Even if your teammates, family, or coaches are pushing you to do something, it won't make a difference. In fact, if you are in this stage and are being pushed you may appear rebellious or insubordinate. A skater who has thought about improving their endurance may be thinking, *I can't improve my endurance,* or *I don't want to improve my endurance.*
2. Contemplation. If you are in this stage, you are thinking about the possibility of achieving your goals. You may be on the fence about it. A skater at this stage could be thinking, *I would like to have better endurance but I'm not sure I want to put the work into it.*
3. Preparation. In this stage of change, you are ready to act and are starting to take small steps. You will be planning how you will accomplish your goal. This could

include determining who will need to be involved, looking at financial aspects, or researching other information. In this stage you will be breaking down your goal into the small, bitesize steps needed to make it happen. A skater in this stage may be thinking, *I am going to start running outside of practice twice a week to have better endurance during games.*

4. Action. This stage of change is all about doing. You know what needs to be done and you are committed to putting it into action. A skater in this stage may say," I have started running outside of practice twice a week so I can have better endurance during games."

5. Maintenance. In this stage you don't have any desire to return to your previous levels of performing. Taking the steps needed to achieve your goals has become a regular part of who you are. You are on an upward climb and intend to keep it going. A skater in this stage may say, "I have been running twice a week for a while now and I like the improvement I see in my endurance during games."

Determine where you are in terms of achieving your roller derby goals. If you are not where you want to be, ask yourself what you can do to tip the scales in favor of change.

# MENTAL TOUGHNESS TOOL
## BE COURAGEOUS: CLIMB A FEAR LADDER

1. Think of something you are afraid to do or try in roller derby.
2. Write that as a goal on the top rung of the Fear Ladder on the next page.
3. Break down your goal into the small steps that will take you to the top.
4. Write the first step on the bottom rung of the ladder. This is something you believe you can do but is a little bit outside of your comfort zone.
5. Write the next step on the rung above that, and so on, until you get to your ultimate goal.

As you take each step, you may feel uncomfortable. Coexist with any emotions or feelings that come up. Do not avoid them or attempt to control them. By approaching, rather than avoiding, potentially uncomfortable, difficult, or even threatening emotions or feelings, you will be able to tolerate distress and move toward your goals.

# MENTAL TOUGHNESS TIP FOR TEAMS #102
## Assess Your Team's Culture

A team's culture, or group identity, is significant because it guides everyone's behaviors and interactions. Culture has to do with the patterns in all that we do as a team. It is the way we practice, the way we play, and the way we socialize. Culture has to do with our attitudes, our habits, our language—our group values. Culture is a learned thing, so a new skater coming in will take on the ways of thinking and acting that were established before them.

The Janssen Sports Leadership Center discusses different types of team cultures, some more negative or positive than others. The first step in building a great team culture is to take an honest look at your team and assess for any problems.

**Corrosive Culture.** This type of toxic team culture has a lot of conflict, negativity, frustration, cliques, gossiping, distrust, and selfishness. There is tension on and off the track. Rather than battling opponents, this type of team spends its time battling each other or the coaches because there is little trust.

**Country Club Culture.** This type of team is all about appearances. There is little accountability, so skaters can coast. Playing time and leadership positions are based on popularity rather than merit. Appearances are more valued than results.

**Congenial Culture.** This team culture focuses on getting along and having harmonious relationships. This group is more interested in being nice than being a high-performance team. Members might not be completely honest in their feedback to each other because they are worried about hurting feelings.

**Comfortable Culture.** This team is interested in doing well but does not push itself beyond its comfort zone. This team has reasonable standards and trains to certain levels, but once things get tough or uncomfortable, they tend to back off. They are a moderately successful team without lifelong bonds.

**Cut-Throat Culture.** In this culture, it is all about results, talent, and success. Character and relationships are often disregarded. All that matters is winning! Team members may end up competing with each other for playing time, coach's attention, and leadership positions which can prevent or destroy relationships when taken too far. If someone is a good skater, their bad attitude will be overlooked.

**Championship Culture.** A team with a championship culture values both relationships and results. They have a strong sense of purpose and commitment to their goals. Team members treat each other with respect and feel worthwhile no matter what their role. Team members willingly put the goals of the team above their own individual goals and take pride in being a part of something bigger than themselves.

Your team may have a combination of these types of cultures. If your team has negative characteristics that aren't aligned with its values, it can be turned into a positive culture with very strong (mentally tough) leadership. Great cultures are built when leaders truly

lead by example. Do your team captains, coaches, and other leaders inspire you with their actions? Great team cultures happen when leaders:
- Demonstrate that rules apply to all, not just to some—things feel fair.
- Treat attitude as being just as principal as physical skills.
- Can keep roller derby in perspective. School, jobs, health, and family always come first.
- Demonstrate that fulfilling the team's mission statement is more valued than the points on the board. They point out the other ways to win.
- Show that they may not always be able to help you achieve your goals, but they won't stop you.
- Empower the other skaters on the team, sharing the leadership.

# MENTAL TOUGHNESS TIP #103
## Prevent Burnout

Burnout will keep you from achieving your best performance. Burnout is defined in *Foundations of Sport and Exercise Psychology* as, "a physical, emotional, and social withdrawal from a formerly enjoyable sport activity." The pressures involved in roller derby can lead to burnout, but they can also be prevented. Below are some ways to prevent roller derby burnout:

**Learn to cope with stress.** There is a general rule for stress: get rid of the stress or get rid of the stressor. If you want to stay involved in roller derby, but find it stressful, then you need to learn how to cope with the stress, so it doesn't lead to burnout.

**Keep training exciting and fun.** It is critical that you are enjoying roller derby since that is really the only reward in our pay-to-play sport. When skaters first join derby they eat it, breathe it, and sleep it. But over time that passion slowly ebbs away. Don't rely on coaches to keep practices fun. It is also your responsibility. You can find ways to make repetitive drills more interesting or challenging by pushing yourself to the next level. Simply being able to avoid taking yourself too seriously, laughing off mistakes, and having a sense of humor can keep practices enjoyable for everyone.

**Reframe unhelpful thinking patterns.** Sometimes the way we think about a situation is what is causing it to be stressful for us. What goes through your head when you think about roller derby?

*I don't want to go to practice tonight.*
or
*I'm going to have a great practice tonight.*

*I can't stand her.*
or
*I'm going to try working together.*

**Stay physically healthy.** The mind and body do not function separately from each other and the state of one will influence the state of the other. When you know you are going to be in mentally stressful situations, be extra vigilant in how you take care of your physical health. Be sure to eat nutritious foods, get adequate sleep, and keep vices under control.

**Take breaks.** Trying to avoid falling behind your competition can lead skaters and teams to set intense, year-round training schedules. It is necessary to take breaks from derby in the same way you take vacations from work.

**Express yourself.** Feelings like disappointment, frustration, and anxiety can become damaging to you if you keep them inside. Expressing these emotions to your teammates, coaches, family, and friends will help you wipe your stress slate clean. Creative activities such as art, journaling, and playing music are other ways to express emotions.

**Focus on short-term goals.** Achieving your derby goals is part of what makes all the hard work and stress worthwhile. Focusing on short-term (achievable within 90 days) rather than long-term goals will help you get to the payoffs faster.

**Develop self-awareness.** Stay in tune with where you're at emotionally and be responsible for yourself. If you're having a tough day maybe it is better to skip practice where things that would normally slide off your back will get under your skin. This is preferable to going to practice and warning teammates, "Stay away from me, I'm in a bad mood." Oversee your own emotions rather than making others take care of them for you. Recognize your signs of stress so you can be proactive and take measures to eliminate it before it becomes a bigger problem.

**Take recovery seriously.** Playing in a game or tournament takes a physical and mental toll on a skater. If you're feeling emotionally drained following a competition, try getting a massage, soaking in a hot tub, watching an enjoyable movie, or minimizing non-derby stressors by taking a day off from work. If you are experiencing mainly physical stressors, try eating more carbohydrates, stretching, sleeping in, or participating in a low-intensity non-derby sport.

*(See page 265 for a stress management technique.)*

# MENTAL TOUGHNESS TIP #104
**Expect the Unexpected**

There are two, segregated brain systems involved in visual attention. The "goal-directed" system is a top-down system that involves us selecting what we want to focus our attention on. The other, "stimulus-driven," bottom-up system, is involved in detecting relevant stimuli in our environment, especially when the stimuli are unexpected and require a behavioral response from us. This second system acts as a "circuit breaker" for the first system, diverting attention to the unexpected event. When we are experiencing anxiety, the stimulus-driven system becomes disrupted, causing us to become aware of more stimuli.

As an illustration, imagine you are skating in the pack during a game or scrimmage, and you are using the top-down, goal-directed part of your brain to keep your eye on the jammer. Then suddenly, the stimulus-driven system detects an opposing blocker about to knock you on your butt. Before you know it, you have lost track of the opposing jammer and they have passed you by. This is an example of how these two controls over our attention are constantly interacting.

How can you improve attentional control in times of high stress? The stimulus-driven system is designed to pick out unusual, surprising things in your environment and force you to divert your attention to them. This is useful for our survival but can get in the way of playing our best. We need to trick this system into turning a "blind eye" to things that would normally require us to act.

Many veteran skaters can do this because they have become accustomed to all the elements of "danger" that are a normal part of roller derby. These skaters can hold a conversation with you about what they are going to make for dinner while simultaneously blocking the jammer and navigating a sweep by an opposing blocker. Their attention on the relevant target remains steadfast through it all.

To improve your attentional control, you will need to condition yourself to expect the unexpected. This can only come from experience, from repeatedly facing situations until they are no longer unusual. You can also skate in a way that is low, stable, protected and ready for anything that comes your way. This will mean minimal behavioral change is necessary; the stimulus-driven system won't fully divert your attention to the new stimulus because you won't need to change much about what you are already doing.

# MENTAL TOUGHNESS TIP #105
## Develop A Healthy Attitude Toward Competition

In *Foundations of Sport and Exercise Psychology*, "achievement motivation" is described as the drive that an individual has to excel, to achieve their goals, to push past obstacles, and to strive for success when being compared to others or with their own past performances. In sports, achievement motivation is often called competitiveness. A skater's state of competitiveness will affect many of their thoughts, feelings, and actions. To see how your achievement motivation influences you, answer the following questions.

1. Do you seek out opponents with equal ability to yourself or do you prefer going up against skaters of much greater or lesser skills?
2. How often do you perform in a situation where you are being evaluated?
3. How much effort do you put into achieving your derby goals? How often do you train outside of practice time?
4. How hard do you try at practice? At how many practices do you take it easy vs. giving it everything you've got?
5. When you face failure or things get tough, do you try harder or back off your efforts?
6. Are you more motivated by achieving success or avoiding failure?
7. Do you attribute successes to things that are within your control? How about failures?

A skater with high achievement motivation, or competitiveness, will have an easy time playing their best and will have the most fun during a tight race that is anyone's game. A skater with low achievement motivation will seek out opponents of much greater ability or much lesser skill so their win or loss will be guaranteed. For them, losing to an evenly matched opponent would be distressing. Those with high achievement motivation seek out difficult challenges and prefer intermediate risks.

High achievers perform well when being evaluated. They think about the possibility of doing well and will look for situations where they can showcase their skills. Low achievers perform worse when they are being evaluated. They are consumed by fears of failure and avoid taking risks.

Athletes with high achievement motivation will put in a lot of work to pursue their goals. They will attend as many practices as possible and put in maximum effort. A skater with low achievement motivation won't put a lot of work toward accomplishing their goals and when the going gets tough will put forward even less effort. High achievers will increase their determination in the face of adversity.

High achievers are motivated by achieving success while low achievers are motivated by wanting to avoid failure. High achievers will attribute success to things within their control (such as effort) and failure to things outside their control (like a tough opponent). Low achievers will attribute success to things outside their control (such as good reffing) and failure to things within their control (like bad game strategy).

This is how you can develop high achievement motivation:

**Assess your attributional style.** Look at what is under your control vs. outside of your control. Learn to let go of those things that are outside of your control and focus your efforts on those things that are under your control. (See page 220 for more information on what is under your control.)

**Consider your personality.** If you are motivated by avoiding failure, push yourself to accept challenges where there is a 50/50 chance of losing. Expose yourself to situations where you will be evaluated.

**Determine who to compete with.** There are times to compete against others and there are times when you should focus on your own individual improvement, essentially competing against yourself.

**Downplay outcome goals.** Instead of only going for the win, concentrate instead on performance and process goals. These will allow you to focus on improving your performance compared to previous performances and help you master the skills needed for success. (See page 178 for more information on giving up attachment to outcomes.)

*(See page 370 for more information on attributional styles.)*

# MENTAL TOUGHNESS TIP #106
## Vision Training To Reduce Concussion

In sports and in life, the mind is everything. Take care of your brain by using vision training to reduce your risk of concussion. Vision training has been shown to reduce incidents of concussion in athletes by improving peripheral vision. Strong peripheral vision allows athletes in full contact sports to increase awareness and avoidance of threats. The University of Cincinnati Division of Sports Medicine has used electronic light board vision training systems for both concussion diagnosis and prevention. This involves an athlete standing in front of a wall of lights and tapping them as fast as possible when they light up.

We can create a low-tech method to improve peripheral vision called "Saccadic Eye Movement Training." A s*accade* refers to the eyes' ability to shift quickly and accurately between targets.

### Four-Square Saccade Exercise
1. Cut out the four saccade charts beginning on page 399. Tape the squares to a wall, 3-4 feet apart from each other.
2. Stand far enough away that you can read all four charts.
3. Read the first letter on the first line from each square, then the second letter from each square, and so on, working all the way through every letter on all four squares until you reach the end.
4. Move only your eyes and not your head.
5. Add unstable surfaces, motor demands, and moving the charts to different places (varying heights, distances) to enhance eye speed and visual focus.

# MENTAL TOUGHNESS TIP #107
## Plan For Poise

To put a consistent effort into your skating, you will need to transform the belief, "I want to skate well, *but* I am angry or frustrated" to "I want to skate well, *and* I am angry or frustrated." The "and" makes all the difference. The first statement indicates emotion-driven actions and the second shows value-driven actions.

Poise means being balanced, level-headed, and in control in the face of difficult emotions that are part of the intense sport of roller derby. If you are always acting in response to how you are feeling or thinking at any given time, your efforts toward success will be inconsistent. You will only do the things necessary for success when you *feel* like doing them. Being poised means doing what you need to do no matter how you are feeling or thinking.

Often, we choose feeling better in the moment over what is best for our derby career. If you use what you value as your guide when choosing your actions and making your decisions, it will help keep you on a steady track to success. Accepting all thoughts and feelings, even the ones you consider to be unbearable or undesirable will help you act in a value-driven way.

Imagine roller derby as a tall mountain you are determined to climb. Your values are at the top of this mountain. They may be Fitness, Health, Fun, Challenge, Risk, Belonging, or Accomplishment. Your roller derby goals are *what* you are working towards, your goal-oriented actions are *how*, but your values are *why*.

During your climb to the top of the mountain, you may experience all kinds of negative, defeating thoughts and feelings. You may doubt you have what it takes, you may worry about getting hurt, or tell yourself you're never going to get there. You may experience emotions such as fear, worry, anxiety, sadness, or frustration. If you listen to the things your mind is telling you as if they were the absolute truth, you would turn back.

Quitting your climb would provide immediate relief for all that inner turmoil, but it would not get you to your goals. By focusing on what is most important to you, you will make steady progress upwards. This is poise: getting the job done despite what is going on in your heart, mind, and body.

Poise requires inner strength and flexibility in how you respond to certain emotionally charged situations. Make a Plan for Poise to deal with the most upsetting moments you encounter in roller derby. What are the situations that make you the angriest or the most frustrated or other performance-interfering emotion? Some examples are hearing negative feedback, having a penalty committed against you, getting a "bad" call, and making a mistake.

Using the Plan for Poise chart, determine how you will remain poised and in control in the face of upsetting thoughts and feelings. Think of some situations that have been problematic for you. What were the negative or upsetting thoughts and emotions associated with that situation? What unhelpful action did you take? Now come up with a personalized plan to take a more helpful action. You may need to confront, rather than avoid, uncomfortable thoughts and feelings.

*(See page 374 for information on taking Opposite Actions.)*

| Problem Situation | Negative Thoughts and Emotions | Unhelpful Actions | Helpful Actions |
|---|---|---|---|
| | | | |
| | | | |
| | | | |

# MENTAL TOUGHNESS TIP #108
## Calibrate Your Sense of Proprioception

Have you ever been given a correction at practice only to think, *Wasn't I doing that?* Or have you received a cut-track penalty and thought, *No way, I was in!* Sometimes our perceptions of what we are doing are different from what we are actually doing. We can use feedback from others to help us calibrate our sense of *proprioception*, or our perception of where our body is in space. Proprioception allows us to control our movements and know how much strength is needed to execute actions. This sense allows humans to control our bodies without needing to directly look at them.

Get your coach or a teammate to help you calibrate your sense of proprioception. At practice, set up a drill for a skill you are working on. Partner up with a teammate and take turns watching each other perform the skill. Immediately after attempting the skill, mentally recall your performance and describe it to them in as much detail as possible. Your partner can then share what they saw. You can adjust your perceptions based on their feedback. Repeat this several times until your perceptions match their observations.

# MENTAL TOUGHNESS TOOL
## BE FIRED UP: BREATH OF FIRE

One of the eight limbs of yoga is *Pranayama,* or the practice of controlling the breath, the source of our vital life force. Breath of Fire is an incredibly effective practice for arriving in the present moment and bringing your mind and body to attention. It delivers oxygen to the brain, resulting in improved focus and a natural state of calm awareness. Breath of Fire also strengthens the nervous system and increases stamina.

This is a powerful practice, so begin with short sessions and stop if you feel dizzy or lightheaded. You can practice this breathing exercise on its own or add it to a yoga pose like plank to really heat things up.

1. Take a comfortable seat, lengthening the spine. Chin is slightly toward your chest.
2. Bring your attention to your Third Eye, just between the brows, with eyes gently closed or gaze softened.
3. Hands can rest on your knees.
4. Take a regular inhale and exhale to begin. Then, inhale halfway and begin breathing rapidly while engaging the belly, letting the belly move in with the exhale and out with the inhale.
5. When you're done, take a deep breath in, hold the air in the back of the throat, and then slowly release the air through the mouth.
6. Sit quietly and observe the effects of this energizing practice.

With Breath of Fire, the breath is rapid, rhythmic and continuous. Inhalations and exhalations are through the nose. Breath is powered from the navel and the solar plexus by rapidly pumping the stomach. On the exhale, air is expelled through the nose by pressing the navel back toward the spine. On the inhale, the belly relaxes, and the diaphragm flattens down. The vacuum created by the exhale will naturally draw air in. This is called a "passive inhalation." Work toward making your inhalations and exhalations equally long. The breath can be fast and rigorous, but the body stays relaxed, especially the face.

As you become more accustomed to this technique, Breath of Fire can be practiced for long periods of time. But to start, a minute or two is good. This is strong stuff that will get you fired up!

# MENTAL TOUGHNESS TIP #109
## Know Your Triggers

Just like we can't control the weather, we may not be able to control the sudden emotional changes that wash over us. However, we can control our responses to those emotions and manage ourselves until the storm passes. Knowing what types of situations cause you to feel upset can help you to prepare yourself. Situations that make us feel rejection, betrayal, humiliation, loss, or fear can bring on extreme emotional responses. Here are some potentially upsetting situations:

- Being provoked
- Losing
- An intense rivalry
- Not playing well

1. If you're expecting rain, bring an umbrella. Anticipate your potential hot button situations and be prepared for them. Rehearse your desired response in your head. What do you want to say or do?

Potentially upsetting situation:

_____

How I responded in the past:

_____

Why was that a problem?

_____

How do I want to respond next time?

_____

2. Even the worst storms eventually pass and so will your current emotional state. Avoid saying or doing something you will regret. Later, when you feel more like yourself, think about what happened. You can try using a process called *emotional honesty*. With this strategy you are honest about what you are feeling and what that emotion tells you about what you need.

*I felt embarrassed when I made a mistake. Then I felt angry because I thought people were laughing at me. Belonging and being accepted is important to me.*

3. Don't blame others for your emotional responses. Sometimes we say things like, "They made me mad." That may be the case, but how you manage that anger is 100% under your control.
4. If you do lose your cool, apologize and try to do better the next time.

# MENTAL TOUGHNESS TOOL
## BE STRONG: WARRIOR II POSE

Warriors are courageous, honorable, disciplined, and compassionate. Warriors have inner and outer strength and a sense of purpose. Embody the qualities of a warrior with this yoga pose which makes you feel strong, steady, and confident.

Stand with legs wide apart. Turn your right foot out so that the heel of the right foot is pointing toward the arch of the left foot. Breathe in and lift your arms up parallel to the earth with palms facing down. Exhale and deeply bend the right knee until it is right over your ankle. Keep your torso centered with shoulders stacked over your hips. Gaze out over your outstretched right hand. Feel yourself standing in your power. Hold for three to five breaths and then switch sides.

As you hold this pose, you could think about your back hand representing your past and your front hand representing your future. We want to be aware of our past and its effect on us, honoring it. At the same time we must remain focused on our future goals, with our eyes looking ahead. We don't want to be stuck in the past or too worried about the future. We keep our weight balanced in the middle, in the present. Alternatively, as you work with this pose, you may choose to reflect on the following questions:
1. Who supports me?
2. Can I be fierce and also in control?
3. How am I strong like a warrior?

# MENTAL TOUGHNESS TIP FOR TEAMS #110
## Practice How You Play
## (because you will play how you practice)

Roller derby games are intense. They are dangerous, thrilling, terrifying, and brutal. Pride may be on the line and adrenaline is pumping. You must be smart, have a positive attitude, and give it everything you've got despite being stressed, excited, exhausted, or frustrated. If the only time your team plays at game levels of intensity is during a game, they are not getting the mental and physical preparation they need to be able to perform at their best during an actual game situation.

It is necessary to have practice time designated for game-like play. This is the time for players to practice giving and receiving hard hits without losing their cool or focus. It is also helpful to learn how to amp up to game play energy levels quickly, despite being tired, grumpy, or not in the mood. By practicing how you want to play, giving 100% effort will feel natural for you and your team.

Here are a couple of things to keep in mind as your practices ramp up the intensity levels. When you get hit hard, don't take it personally. To ask your teammate to pull back is to ask them to sacrifice their own growth. Remind yourself how glad you are that they are on *your* team!

It can be difficult for all to get their energy levels up to game-level if there are inconsistent energy levels among those present. A few may be giving it everything they've got, a few may be just going through the motions, and the rest are probably somewhere in the middle. Set up expectations and rituals for getting everyone amped up to play their best at practice.

1. Leave any stressors (derby or non-derby) outside the door.
2. Be prepared to go into battle, just like game day.
3. Have a team ritual or warm up designed for amping up.
4. Practice with 100% effort and expect your teammates to do the same.

The more elements you can create that replicate an actual game experience, the more prepared, mentally and physically, your team will be on game day.

*Anything worth doing is worth doing well.*

# MENTAL TOUGHNESS TIP FOR FRESH MEAT #111
## Survive and Thrive In Your First Game

Being in your first few games can be a daunting experience. Your teammates are shouting instructions at you. Your coach is giving you directions. Friends, family, and strangers are watching you from the audience. The opposing team is trying to kill you. It is a new, high-pressure situation and you may be just trying not to die! All of this is going to trigger your fight or flight response. This means your short-term memory, concentration, and rational thought are all going to be suppressed. The stress response process evolved to allow you to give your attention completely to the task at hand (to repel or flee from a threat).

Knowing that this is what is happening with you, the best way to deal with it is to focus on only one thing when you go out on the track. For example, just stick with one of your teammates (who can give you guidance). Coaches and veteran teammates should be aware of the mental state of their newbs and avoid giving them a long list of instructions to follow. Keep it simple and stick to one thing at a time. Using this strategy will lead to less frustration and a more positive experience for everyone on the team.

Once you have a bunch of games under your belt this stress response will lessen. You will become a "big picture" player who can see beyond the immediate moment.

# MENTAL TOUGHNESS TOOL
## BE POWERFUL: COBRA POSE

The figure of the serpent has symbolized the power that is within everyone. The shedding of skin is seen to represent transformation and renewal. Many people are afraid of snakes. When a snake's head moves, the movement is transmitted all the way through its body to the tail.

Lie on your belly with the tops of your feet pressed into the earth and legs hip-distance apart. Your fingers will be pointing straight ahead with palms down. Press into your hands, inhale, and lift your head, heart, and belly. The tops of your feet will remain pressed into the earth with your knees engaged. Your eyes will look up. Hold for three breaths, lower slowly and repeat two more times.

As you work with Cobra pose, you may reflect on the following questions:
1. How can I shed my old skin?
2. Am I leading with my head?
3. Where does my power come from?

# MENTAL TOUGHNESS TOOL
## BE DRIVEN: MY DREAM GOAL EXERCISE

This method of goal setting is fun and unique because you get to start with your loftiest dream goal and work backwards to a tangible step you can take today.

---

**My Dream Goal**

1. My dream goal is _____

_____

2. In one year I will _____

_____

3. In six months I will _____

_____

4. In one month I will _____

_____

5. In one week I will _____

_____

6. Today I will _____

_____


**Signature/Date:**

X_____

# MENTAL TOUGHNESS TIP #112
## Change Your Story

The beliefs you hold to be true about yourself as an athlete determine your story. This story, in turn, drives your actions. Our beliefs come from our biology and our experiences. There are three realms for our beliefs as athletes: our beliefs about ourselves, our beliefs about our future, and our beliefs about others. These underlying beliefs, or world views, are known as *schemas.*

Interestingly, people will work very hard to make sure things fit into their schemas, even if there is evidence to the contrary. If one's schema is a healthy one, with elements of self-efficacy, self-determination, and optimism, this works out well. If your schema includes themes of mistrust, self-doubt, and doom, it is going to be difficult to fulfill your potential. Take an honest look at your beliefs about yourself as an athlete.

My beliefs about myself:

_____


My beliefs about my future:

_____

My beliefs about others:

_____

Do you notice any areas that you would like to change? Since beliefs are formed through our experiences, having new experiences can change our beliefs. We can create the type of experiences that will be helpful in rewriting our schema by taking actions that are aligned with what we want to believe.

If your underlying belief system is problematic, take the steps below to change it:

1. Determine what you want to believe. This is your target belief or schema. Make this something you can stand behind. Don't choose something unbelievable or unrealistic.

a. I want to believe this about myself as an athlete:

_____

b. I want to believe this about my future as an athlete:

_____

c. I want to believe this about others in my sport:

_____

2. Write down one action that you would take for each target area if you truly believed it:

a. _____

b. _____

c. _____

    Taking new actions will change your story about yourself as an athlete. You can alter your deep-rooted, underlying belief system just by living in a new way!

# MENTAL TOUGHNESS TIP FOR FEMALES #113
**Train Like A Woman**

It's time to end the stigma around periods. Half the women in the world menstruate. It's not dirty, shameful, something to hide, or something to be embarrassed by. And since it is shown that periods affect sports performance, this is even more reason to end the taboo and talk openly about the subject. The paper, "Sports, Exercise, and the Menstrual Cycle" published in the *British Journal of Sports Medicine,* found over half the elite athletes questioned reported their menstrual cycle affected their training and performance. When you have an understanding and solutions, you can be at your best no matter what time of the month it is!

Menstruation, or a period, is a natural process of vaginal bleeding that occurs as part of a female's monthly cycle. Every month, your body prepares for pregnancy. If no pregnancy occurs, the uterus, or womb, sheds its lining. Cycles can range between 21 and 45 days. Periods typically last between 3 and 7 days and blood loss can vary. Pre-menstrual symptoms (PMS) can occur 5-10 days prior to the start of your period and include:

- Insomnia and headaches
- Bloating, constipation, and diarrhea
- Breast tenderness
- Fatigue
- Irritability
- Emotional tenderness
- Joint or muscle pain

Symptoms usually go away once your period starts, but then you may have mild to severe cramping and some experience very heavy bleeding. Being worried about starting your period or leaking if you have a period with a heavy flow can sap confidence and cause insecurities on the track. Not having the tools to handle the hormonal changes your system goes through daily can lead to feelings of confusion or helplessness. Knowing there are specific ways you can train like a woman can be empowering. The guidance below comes from the fitrwoman app which tracks cycles and provides training and nutritional information that is relevant for where you are at.

**Phase 1:** During your period your estrogen and progesterone levels will be at their lowest. Your cognitive functioning will be high. This is a great time to learn new, complex skills that require a lot of coordination. At this point it's beneficial to build strength so focus your training on strength and high intensity interval training. You may be able to push yourself harder during this phase. Increased inflammation may hinder recovery so give yourself adequate time to rest. Exercise can reduce menstrual symptoms and relieve tension. Be sure to warm up with muscle activation exercises first since neuromuscular control might be lower. Eat carbohydrates to fuel your training if working on endurance. Restore iron levels by consuming iron-rich foods along with sources of vitamin C. Symptoms can be reduced by increasing antioxidants, anti-inflammatory foods, and those rich in vitamin D, calcium, fish oils, and B vitamins.

**Phase 2:** Just before ovulation, estrogen levels are rising to a peak and progesterone levels are still very low. You may feel increasingly happy, positive, alert and have more energy. With blood sugar levels stabilizing, your appetite may decrease. You might find your pain threshold higher and that you can push yourself harder. This is the time to maximize your high intensity and strength training. Recovery is better during this phase which will help with muscle tissue repair following intense training, but be sure to warm up and warm down. Prioritize recovery by allowing at least 48 hours to recover from an intense training session. Continue to fuel your training with carbohydrates but towards the end of this phase emphasize healthy fats for moderate and low intensity exercise. Eat sources of collagen and vitamin rich foods to help with soft tissue recovery. Include protein and carbohydrates in your recovery drink or snack as soon as possible after training.

**Phase 3:** Estrogen levels fall during ovulation and some might feel some pain. After this, both estrogen and progesterone levels start to rise. You may feel reduced strength during this phase. Appetite, heart rate, and body temperature can increase, and immunity can decrease. Blood sugar levels may be unstable leading to cravings. You may feel more emotional and empathetic. This is the time to focus on moderate intensity endurance training. If your energy levels and strength are not high you can lower the intensity levels and power demands of your training. This is also a great time to work on improving flexibility, agility, and footwork. Fuel your training with healthy fats (e.g. avocado, cashews) for moderate and low intensity exercise. Refuel with a protein rich snack within 30 minutes of training to help repair muscle breakdown. To address unstable blood sugar levels, include protein with every meal and eat snacks with complex carbohydrates (e.g. beans, vegetables, whole grains). Remember to hydrate for extended endurance training.

**Phase 4:** Now estrogen and progesterone levels are at their lowest point. This drop causes an inflammatory response which is thought to be the cause of PMS symptoms. This can affect your ability to recover after an intense training session. With falling hormones and rising metabolic rate, your appetite and cravings may increase. You might have sleep difficulties during this phase which can affect your concentration, alertness, and performance. Stress has been found to make PMS symptoms worse so do what you can to relax. All types of training are good during this phase as exercise has anti-inflammatory and antioxidant properties that can reduce PMS and boost your mood. You may not feel motivated to exercise during this phase, but consider taking advantage of this simple, free, and natural treatment option. As this phase ends, the body will switch from using fats to carbohydrates for fueling training. Focus on eating slow release carbohydrates to maintain blood sugar levels and reduce cravings. Avoid saturated fats, caffeine, and alcohol which may make PMS worse.

Below are some more tips for training like a woman:
1. Track your cycles so you know what is currently happening in your body because of daily, changing hormone levels. Team sports can't change training for one person, but you should know what to focus on during certain times of the month.

2. Try out a variety of period products. This is a rapidly growing market as more and more women are becoming activists in this area and expanding our options. Be prepared by keeping extra products available to all in your team's bout bag.
3. Talk with your teammates about their experiences, sharing tips and rants.
4. If periods are a big problem for you, you can talk to your doctor about the possibility of managing them with oral contraceptives. These have helped some women by making their periods lighter and regular with less symptoms.
5. For those with heavy periods it is important to rule out anemia which causes fatigue, shortness of breath, chest pain, and fainting.

Some female athletes report that they perform even better than usual around the beginning of their period, experiencing extra energy and a bit more aggression than usual. A period is not a curse. It is a sign of your strength and your power.

# MENTAL TOUGHNESS TIP #114
## Tame The Envy

Have you ever felt jealous, threatened, or envious of the success of a teammate? Perhaps you were the top dog on your team and then a new skater joined whose juking leaves you in the dust? Or you joined derby at the same time as another skater who has already passed all their minimum skill requirements way before you? Jealousy is often driven by insecurity and self-doubt. It can come from the belief that if others are great, then we aren't. Part of what makes a great team is great skaters, and the more, the better! Learning to be truly happy for others and transforming jealousy into genuine admiration and inspiration is a worthwhile goal. In the meantime, learn how to manage this difficult emotion.

Have you heard the phrase, "green with envy"? It exemplifies how this emotion can bring out our worst. Jealousy or envy, when we act on it, can turn us into monsters. On the next page, draw your green, envy monster. Then add something to the picture as a reminder that you have power over this aspect of yourself. Below are some ideas. Get creative! Don't forget to give your monster a name.

- Attach a leash or draw it in a cage
- Give it a silly accessory such as a funny hat
- Draw a cuddly friend or a snack to soothe it

Next time you feel this strong emotion rising, remind yourself, this is my green monster and I can control it.

# MENTAL TOUGHNESS TIP #115
## Don't Make Excuses

Mentally tough athletes don't make excuses when things don't go their way. They take responsibility for their own performance. Blaming others or uncontrollable elements of a situation is a waste of time. Focus on what you can control. Determine what needs to be adjusted and come back fighting.

Think of the last time you lost a game. Did you make excuses? Here are some common ones:
- Slippery floor
- Having a health condition
- Bad calls from officials
- Opposing skaters not playing fair
- Your jammer goes to the box in the last jam

Within each of these areas of blame are places where a skater can take control and be accountable. No excuses!

**Slippery floor.** Find out ahead of time what the surface is you will be skating on. Be prepared with the right wheel hardness. Or better yet, always bring an assortment of wheels and practice on all types of surfaces.

**Having a health condition.** Sometimes people say or think they can't accomplish greatness because they have a mental or physical condition. But this isn't a hard truth. An athlete can rise to the top, despite facing challenges, setbacks, and adversity. You may have to work harder than others to get there, but it is possible. Keep your focus on your abilities rather than on your limitations. Your situation can make you determined to never give up on your goals. You may do well *because* of what you have been through or are going through, not *despite* it.

**Bad calls from officials.** Flexible thinking is useful here. Perhaps the official is seeing something you're not aware of. Or maybe you're correct and they are out to get you. In that case, it is up to you to play extra clean and smart. (See page 166 for more on being cognitively flexible.)

**Opposing skaters not playing fair.** This is a time where acceptance is useful. Shit happens. Things are going to go down on the track that are outside of the parameters of the rules of game play. Accept it, develop strategies to prevent if from interfering with your game, and move on.

**Your jammer goes to the box in the last jam.** Putting too much blame or pressure on your jammer during the last jam can be unfair. There were 58 minutes or more of game play prior to that last jam where a score that close could have been avoided. Looking at the game as a whole is more productive.

Always do the best that you can on any given day. When you're up against a challenge, you're going to find lots of reasons why you couldn't do it. Evaluate which ones are real and handle them. Determine which ones are excuses and eliminate them.

# MENTAL TOUGHNESS TIP #116
## Be Your Own Cheerleader

Sometimes we are our own worst enemy. We tell ourselves horrible things such as, *I don't deserve to be here*, *I'm not good enough*, or *That was stupid*.

The term for the things we tell our self is "self-talk." Self-talk has a huge impact on our performance because we believe what we hear, even if that message is coming from inside our own head. Negative self-talk can fuel anger, frustration, and extreme anxiety. These emotional states affect our breathing, increase muscle tension, and create a loss of concentration which results in lower performance. On the other hand, if an athlete's self-talk is positive and relevant, this leads to an emotional experience of relaxation, calmness, and feeling centered. As a result, athletes who use positive self-talk are going to perform better.

Negative self-talk typically occurs following a mistake or other situation where you feel emotionally vulnerable. Negative self-talk is distracting mental chatter that gets in the way of playing your best. Negative self-talk can include mean words or pessimistic predictions like these:

*Nobody wants me here.*
*Everyone's faster than me.*
*I'm going to lose the game for us.*

Be your own cheerleader and give yourself realistic encouragement and motivation. Avoid harsh, tough, motivational talk that bullies you into submission (*Come on, don't be a _____!*). Great self-talk puts you in a positive emotional state. One that is ready to take on the task at hand—strong, energized, determined, and focused. Positive self-talk allows you to enjoy the game more. Say the following positive statements to yourself and see how it makes you feel:

*Own it!*
*Work hard!*
*Try your best!*

Replace negative self-talk with positive self-talk and watch your game improve.

| Negative Self-talk | Positive Self-talk |
|---|---|
| *Wow, that was sucky.* | *Reset and try again.* |
| *I'll never get there.* | *Focus on the small steps.* |

Now write down some of your own negative self-talk and replace it with something positive, encouraging, and motivational.

| Negative Self-talk | Positive Self-talk |
|---|---|
| | |
| | |
| | |

To test out whether your self-talk is positive or negative, ask yourself if you would talk like that to one of your teammates.

# MENTAL TOUGHNESS TIP #117
## Avoid Unhelpful Thinking Styles

*Cognitive distortions* are ways that our mind convinces us of things. These thinking styles are often automatic and subconscious. Below are some unhelpful thinking styles that reinforce negative thinking. Which of these do you tend to do?

**All-or-nothing thinking:** This is sometimes called black and white thinking.

*If I'm not perfect, I failed.*

**Mental filter:** Only paying attention to certain types of evidence, usually the negative types.

*See? I suck.*

**Mind reading:** Jumping to conclusions by imagining we know what others are thinking.

*They don't want me here.*

**Fortune telling:** This is another way to jump to conclusions. Here we predict the future.

*We're gonna lose.*

**Emotional reasoning:** Assuming that if we feel a certain way then what we think is true.

*I feel embarrassed so what I did was embarrassing.*

**Labelling:** Assigning labels to ourselves or others.

*I'm an idiot.*

**Overgeneralizing:** Seeing a pattern based on a single event or making overly broad conclusions.

*We always do that.*

**Catastrophizing:** Blowing something out of proportion.

*That was the worst reffing EVER!*

**Personalization:** Blaming yourself or taking responsibility for something that wasn't completely your fault.

*We lost because of me.*

**The Shoulds:** Using critical words like "should" or "must" can make us feel guilty or frustrated.

*They shouldn't act that way.*

**Disqualifying the positive:** Discounting the good things you have done.

*That doesn't count.*

Notice when you are using unhelpful thinking styles. The first step to change is self-awareness.

*(Learn more about the Shoulds on page 182.)*

# MENTAL TOUGHNESS TIP #118
**Find Strength While Injured**

Being an athlete means focusing on your strengths. When you get injured, you are forced to explore your weaknesses, maybe for the first time. This can be a devastating experience. One way to help you get through it is to allow yourself the full range of human emotions. A skater can experience many of the following after an injury:
- Guilt
- Frustration
- Loneliness
- Anger
- Hopelessness
- Identity loss
- Fears
- Depression
- Anxiety
- Doubts
- Lack of confidence
- Nightmares

Feel angry, scared, or sad if that is where you're at. Experiencing the emotions, rather than denying them, will help you to move through them in a growth-oriented way. Emotions such as sadness can feel vulnerable. This is a time when you can tap into your emotional strength, giving you the ability to sit with uncomfortable or painful feelings. Sometimes the only way out is through.

You are a strong, worthwhile athlete, whether you are injured or not. Find other ways to define being an athlete that aren't dependent on your present ability to skate. Live like an athlete every day while you are injured, and you will only have the physical aspects of recovery to come back from.

Being an athlete means:
- Having the guts to show up and finish something
- Striving to improve
- Having dedication, focus, and a strong work ethic
- Being single-minded in pursuits
- Having a sense of commitment
- A willingness to make sacrifices

Use imagery to practice while you are injured without ever having to lace up your skates. You can go over skills drills, work on plays, develop strategies, and more. Mental practice sends the same messages between your brain and body as physical practice does. Using imagery to continue to train while off your skates will speed your ability to get rolling once healed.

*Find a more powerful way to define yourself. You are an athlete still!*

# MENTAL TOUGHNESS TOOL
## BE POISED: INOCULATE YOURSELF AGAINST STRESS

This guided meditation, adapted with permission from *The iRest Program for Healing PTSD*, can enhance your experience of joy by increasing your willingness to experience moderate doses of stress. Treat each stressful life event you encounter as an opportunity to vaccinate yourself against stress and strengthen your ability to welcome and experience joy.

With your eyes gently open or closed, welcome the environment and sounds around you. The touch of air on your skin, the sensations where your body touches the surface that's supporting it, your body breathing, the various sensations that are present throughout your body.
Now locate the felt-sense of joy in your body. You may feel joy in any number of ways, as the feeling of connection, well-being, contentment, peace, enthusiasm, or some other sensation particular to your body and mind. As you locate the felt-sense of joy in your body, sense where and how you experience it. Perhaps it is a warm feeling in your heart or a gentle smile on your face or a glow in your belly that radiates out to your arms and legs. Welcome the feeling of joy, however you experience it in your body and mind. If it is helpful, bring to mind a memory of a person, animal, place, or object that brings a sense of joy into your body. Allow the feeling of joy to grow and spread throughout your body.
Now pair the feeling of joy with a negative sensation, emotion, or thought, or with a stressor you're

experiencing. Whether a situation, image or memory, feel how this stressful thought, emotion, or situation affects your body and mind.

Now alternate between experiencing the felt-sense of joy and the negative stressor. Go back and forth, alternating by first feeling joy in your body, then the negative stressor in your body.

Now take time to feel both at the same time, joy and stress, joy and the negative stressor. Allow joy to spread throughout your body even as you're feeling the negative stress.

Then when it feels right, let go of the negative stressor and come back to just feeling joy spreading throughout your body and mind. Rest here for as long as you feel comfortable.

When you're ready to complete this practice, let your eyes open and close several times as you welcome the felt-sense of joy to accompany you throughout your day and life.

# MENTAL TOUGHNESS TIP #119
## Turn Weaknesses Into Strengths

The dichotomous nature of things means anything, and everything, holds opposing truths. Our strengths can be weaknesses and our weaknesses can be strengths. For example, independence can be a strength, but too much independence means we might not work well with others or accept feedback when we need it.

Fear can be a weakness, but some fear is necessary because it protects us from danger, helping us to gauge risks or alerting us to threats. Being impulsive can be a weakness because you may get insubordination penalties for mouthing off to officials. This same impulsiveness can make you an effective jammer because you will go for holes without considering the risks.

By learning to use your weaknesses for your benefit, you will realize you can release yourself from negative judgment and transcend the nature of duality.

1. Write down one of your personal qualities that you consider to be a weakness.

_____

2. How has this hurt you, or held you back, in derby?

_____

_____

3. Determine how you can use this weakness to help you in your derby game, effectively turning this into a strength.

_____

_____

# MENTAL TOUGHNESS TIP #120
## Know When To Say When

Many serious injuries happen when an athlete plays past the point of exhaustion or pain. The pressure competitive sports puts on individuals to always give 110% makes an athlete feel like they are weak if they ask for a break. It may be treated as a betrayal to your team to put anything above your sport, including your health.

Why is this? Sports psychologists posit that sport culture minimizes the importance of injuries and promotes the idea of playing through pain. Coaches and athletes may give those who play through injury respect and accolades. Athletes may even be told that this is something that is expected of them if they want to make it. Studies show those who have higher athletic identity are more likely to think playing through pain and injury is a good thing. Not only do these athletes minimize the risk of pain or injury, they see it as a necessary part of the sport, take pride in it, and don't fear it. Sound familiar?

Roller derby is notorious for glamorizing the physical brutality of the sport. Think of the many skater names and team names that exude violence or threat. Or consider league websites that feature a "Hall of Pain," showcasing particularly gruesome bruises or other injuries worn by skaters as a badge of honor.

Let's assume that many roller derby participants do think positively about playing through pain and injury. Is this so bad? In the moment, you help your team, perhaps accomplish some amazing feats, and maybe feel that electrifying rush of a win.

Yet, some athletes choose not to push through pain and injury. If you are interested in breaking out of the culture of pain, here are some suggestions to help:

1. Think about yourself as a capable, healthy athlete across your entire lifetime. If you use it all up now, you won't have anything left except endless days of chronic pain.

2. Be able to distinguish between the normal discomfort accompanying hard training and game play from the pain accompanying the onset of injuries. An awareness of the difference can help you know when to say when.

3. Be prepared for some pushback. The existence of a culture of risk, pain, and injury is a real thing in sports. Doing something that goes against the grain will be challenging.

*When in doubt, sit it out.*

# MENTAL TOUGHNESS TIP #121
## Bridge The Gap Between Practice And Play

Athletes may notice a difference between their performance at practices and games. This usually comes down to an inability on the part of the skater to deal with the added pressures of competition. The problem is not a lack of physical skills, but mental skills. The solution is to make practice more like play.

Elite athletes may arrive to game locations days ahead of time to allow acclimation to the conditions. This is probably not possible for most teams, but you can *psychologically* advance the venue. Find photos or videos that show the floor, track set up, what the lighting is like, where the teams sit, how the audience is set up, etc. When you walk through the venue doors it will feel like you've already been there.

Bring as many game elements as possible into your practices ahead of game day:
1. Wear your bout-fits including any war paint.
2. Invite family and friends to create an audience.
3. Use the same warm up you will use at the game.
4. Follow game structure including penalties, time between jams, coach location and actions, and team seating.

Become desensitized to the differences between practice and play by getting accustomed to game elements. This will decrease game day stress, anxiety, and distractions.

# MENTAL TOUGHNESS TOOL
## BE FOCUSED: FOCUS TRAINING EXERCISE II

This exercise will increase your ability to pay attention to the task at hand. To be mentally tough, it is necessary to be able to focus on what is needed to get the job done, no matter how tough the job.

Think about a roller derby performance situation that caused you to experience very strong negative emotions such as anger, anxiety, fear, or worry. Put yourself back in that situation. Where do you feel the emotions in your body? What were you thinking about? Once you are having the same thoughts and feelings you were at that time, complete this task:
1. Think about an upsetting roller derby situation.
2. Stand up and balance on one foot for 30 seconds.
3. Try to be as steady as possible.

After the 30 seconds have passed, reflect on what you needed to focus on to do this task successfully. Were you able to shift your attention from upsetting thoughts and feelings to what was relevant to completing this task? Did you notice any negative or irrelevant thoughts and feelings coming into your head during this exercise? If so, were you able to gently shift your focus back to the present moment and the task?

Next you are going to repeat this activity, except you will imagine you are balancing on a tree branch that extends out ten feet above a river.
1. Think about an upsetting roller derby situation.
2. Stand up, close your eyes and balance on one foot for thirty seconds. Imagine you are balancing on a tree branch that extends out ten feet above a river.
3. Try to be as steady as possible.

Evaluate any changes in your ability to easily shift your focus between your internal experience of the past to the present task at hand. Was it more difficult to do as the (imaginary) stakes for the task went up? How well do you think you could do this if you really were standing on a tree branch high above the water? Would your thoughts and fears overwhelm you? Would you be able to focus on what you need to be successful?

Last, you are going to repeat all the above except you will complete ten jumping jacks first to make you feel some of the physiological sensations (increased heart rate) that come along with feeling upset.
1. Think of an upsetting roller derby situation.
2. Do ten jumping jacks.
3. Close your eyes and balance on one foot for thirty seconds. Imagine you are balancing on a tree branch that extends out ten feet above a river.
4. Try to be as steady as possible.

How did you do that time? Jumping jacks increase your heart rate which can trigger the mind-body stress feedback loop by sending messages to the brain that something is wrong. Our mind-body stress feedback loop is activated when our system, detecting a threat, sends a message to our nervous system which causes alarming feelings. To be successful at this task, you must tolerate distressing physical sensations that often go along with negative thoughts and feelings. You need to shift your focus away from them to what is relevant to successfully completing the task at hand.

# MENTAL TOUGHNESS TIP #122
## Manage Your Emotions

Have you ever heard someone use their emotions as an excuse as to why they did or didn't do something?

"I didn't try it because I was scared."
"I didn't mean to say that, but I was so angry."

Emotions are not the problem. It is our reactions to our emotions that get in the way of fulfilling our potential. With practice, everyone can improve their ability to manage their emotions. Typically, if one is experiencing an emotion such as anger or frustration, there is energy that needs to be released. If this is not managed, a skater may do or say something they regret such as yelling at a team member. If one is experiencing an emotion such as fear, there is a heightened state that needs to be soothed. If this is not managed, a skater may become overwhelmed and unable to act.

Write down some releasing activities you can do at a practice or a game. One idea has been provided:

1. Lion's Breath (see page 175).


2.


3.

Write down some soothing activities you can do at a practice or a game. One idea has been provided.

1. Child Pose (see page 345).

2.

3.

# MENTAL TOUGHNESS TOOL
## BE PREPARED: CREATE A WINNING ROUTINE

Your routine is like a funnel that focuses you in the right direction and on the right things. Your game routine can include meals, gear, uniform, music, mental and physical activities, and more. Your routine will evolve over time. Keep in mind, flexibility is key. Don't put so much emphasis on your routine that you become unable to perform if some part is missing. Part of being a mentally tough athlete is being able to adapt to unexpected or undesirable situations and still be able to give 100%.

Sports psychologist Jennifer Etnier, in her book, *Bring You're 'A' Game*, writes that a good pre-game routine will warm up your body, help you to achieve the appropriate energy level, and assist you to focus on the essential aspects of the game. Etnier also suggests athletes develop a post-game routine to help them deal with the emotions they may be experiencing following a competition. In the event of an upsetting loss, it is essential to take the time to get control of your emotions and behavior, focus on the positive aspects of the game, and prepare to respond in a positive way to fans, friends, opposing team, family, and teammates.

Create a winning routine on the following page. This template begins 24 hours prior to game time, but you can begin your game routine much earlier. Include all the necessary elements for getting into your best state, mentally and physically. Establish a different pre-game routine for home and away games. In between games, review your routine to see if there is anything you want to adjust.

| Day/Time | Activity |
|---|---|
| 24 hours pre-game | |
| 10 hours pre-game | |
| 6 hours pre-game | |
| 3 hours pre-game | |
| 2 hours pre-game | |
| 1 hour pre-game | |
| 15 minutes pre-game | |
| Post-game | |
| 1 day post-game | |

# MENTAL TOUGHNESS TOOL
## BE CENTERED: STILL WATER GUIDED MEDITATION

Begin by closing your eyes and focusing on your breathing. Place all your attention and concentration on your breathing. Take five slow, deep breaths, and notice how relaxed you feel as you exhale.

Using your imagination, visualize that you are sitting comfortably on a chair at the edge of a mountain lake. It is early morning and it is very quiet. You have the whole place to yourself. Take a slow, deep breath, and using your mind's eye, look at the body of water. As you look at the water, notice the ripples on the surface. These ripples are symbolic of stress in your mind and body. They represent distracting thoughts, stress, frustrations or just nervous energy. With each breath, recognize what these thoughts, feelings or sensations might be, and let one dissolve as you exhale. Still using your mind's eye to view the mountain lake, sense that this body of water is like your body. As you let go of these distracting thoughts, notice that the surface of the water is becoming calm. Take several more slow, deep breaths, letting things go as you exhale. Notice with each slow, deep breath that the surface of the lake becomes calmer, beginning to reflect everything around it, like a big mirror. Using your imagination, begin to see a mirror image on the surface of the lake, revealing the trees along the lake shore, the clear blue sky above, and perhaps a snow-covered mountain in the distance.

*"Do you have the patience to wait until your mud settles and the water is clear?"*
*- Lao Tzu, Tao Te Ching*

# MENTAL TOUGHNESS TIP #123
## Grow Positive Seeds

According to Hindu and Buddhist teachings, a part of our mind called the *store conscious* or *mind-field* is planted with seeds known as *bijas*. There are both positive and negative bijas here, sown by our family, teachers, friends, and society. There are seeds of happiness, hope, sadness, fear, and anger. Every day our thoughts, words, and actions plant new seeds in this field of our consciousness and what these seeds grow into become the stuff of our lives.

Thich Nhat Hanh, spiritual leader, peace activist, poet, and mindfulness expert, teaches us how we can choose to grow the positive seeds. When you plant wheat, wheat will grow. Therefore, if you plant seeds of strength, strength will grow. If you act fearful, cowardice will grow. Mindfulness practice helps us identify all the seeds in our consciousness and then we can choose which ones we want to water.

1. Seeds take time to grow. Be patient. Just as when you plant a seed in a garden, you won't see the results immediately. Focus on the positives and you will see the evidence of the progress you are making.
2. Be aware of the negatives. Acknowledge where they come from and that they exist. However, they don't serve you now and you can let them be. Paying too much attention to them will cause them to grow but ignoring doesn't work either.
3. Seeds must change to grow. Embrace the transformation that is happening, even if it is scary or painful at times—beautiful flowers are growing!

# MENTAL TOUGHNESS TIP #124
## Give Yourself Affirmations

In his book, *Creative Coaching*, sports psychologist Jerry Lynch defines an affirmation as, "a strong, positive, concise phrase that states one's goals and directions." The words athletes tell themselves have the power to predict the future. They make a difference in how an athlete feels, emotionally and physically. Positive words can make an athlete feel energized, powerful, and motivated. Negative words can make one feel defeated before they even begin by creating anxiety and self-doubt. Here are some examples of affirmations:

*I am constantly improving*
*I hit like a wrecking ball*
*I am in control and ready to roll*
*I'm a rock star*
*I am here, now*
*I am healthy, worthwhile, and strong*
*I achieve success every day*

Write a different affirmation for the different aspects of derby so you are prepared for every situation. Affirmations should be short, simple, and positive. They should state what you want, not what you don't want. Be sure to use the present tense. This will help you act as if the future is now. Once you have your affirmations written down, say them out loud every day and act as if they are true.

## My Affirmations

Self-image: _____

Ability: _____

Opponents: _____

Confidence: _____

Concentration: _____

Injury: _____

Goals: _____

Other: _____

Other: _____

# MENTAL TOUGHNESS TIP #125
## Act On Impulse

Mel Robbins, author of *The 5-Second Rule*, offers a way to make you unstoppable. To use the 5-second rule, push yourself out of your head and into action by counting down 5-4-3-2-1 and then taking immediate action toward one of your goals or toward whatever you are thinking of. Five seconds doesn't allow your thinking brain to get involved. Your actions will come from your heart and your instinct. In five seconds, you can be courageous by acting on impulse instead of overthinking and possibly being overtaken by fear.

*Don't think, do!*

# MENTAL TOUGHNESS TIP #126
## Use Imagery To Correct Mistakes

As a derby skater, you are constantly getting corrections from your coaches and teammates. Hear what they tell you and then incorporate that feedback into an image in your mind that allows you to really see and feel the skill being executed correctly.

When your coach gives you feedback or when you realize on your own that you made a mistake, immediately follow these steps to correct yourself.

1. Listen. Take the time to understand what you need to do differently.
2. See. Close your eyes and immediately see yourself in your mind performing the skill correctly.
3. Feel. Be in your body as you imagine yourself. Feel the muscles needed to execute the skill engage. Notice how your weight needs to shift. Sense where your body needs to be in space.

# MENTAL TOUGHNESS TOOL FOR TEAMS
## BE FOCUSED: PASS THE STAR

An external focus of attention is crucial when a star pass is being attempted. This is an on-skates game you can do with your team.

1. Create two teams. Pick two jammers. One will continuously lap the pack and the other will remain in the pack, repeatedly passing the star.
2. For the jammer who is lapping the pack: This jammer will lap the pack as many times as possible. For the in-pack jammer: This jammer will never leave the pack, only pass the star.
3. When they are ready, the in-pack jammer will take off the star and pass it to a skater on their team. It can be passed to any skater, not just the pivot. There are no "pass backs," meaning the star can't be passed directly back to the skater who it was passed from. The star is passed by legal means, but not put on the helmet. The star will be passed as many times as possible. It is helpful to have someone off-track do the counting.
4. You can do this drill for one to two minutes and then switch roles. Discuss what skaters were focused on or distracted by. What can be done to improve focus on the relevant elements of the task?

# MENTAL TOUGHNES TOOL
## BE COURAGEOUS: RISK TAKING CHALLENGE

Get out of your comfort zone and into the magic zone! Risk taking leads to success. When you take conscious risks, it reinforces the belief that you are brave. When you believe you are brave, you will take more risks.

Below is a challenge to take some non-roller derby risks. When you try one, notice the emotional and physiological sensations you experience. They may be the same as if you are risking your physical safety, though these are only emotional risks.

1. Admit that you don't know the answer.
2. Go somewhere new.
3. Express your true viewpoint.
4. Tell someone you appreciate them.
5. Ask for something you don't think you'll get.
6. Give an impromptu public speech.
7. Negotiate with someone.
8. Publicly state your biggest goal.
9. Give away something special.
10. Speak up when you see something wrong.
11. Try a new activity.
12. Take on a physical challenge that sounds impossible.
13. Allow yourself to be judged.
14. Make a gut decision.
15. Try a different social scene.
16. Wear something a little crazy.
17. Talk to a complete stranger.
18. Randomly start dancing or singing.

# MENTAL TOUGHNESS TIP #127
**Prevent Burnout With The 4 A's**

Use the Four A's: avoid, alter, adapt, and accept, to deal with stress and prevent roller derby burnout.

**AVOID:** Try to minimize the stressors. This means learning to say "no" and figuring out the difference between "shoulds" and "musts."

**ALTER:** If you can't avoid the stressor, then try to change it. Speak up about things that are bothering you and let your emotions out (appropriately).

**ADAPT:** If you can't avoid or alter the stressor, then try to change you. Change the way you look at things to keep derby a positive experience. Focus on the areas of this sport that you really love.

**ACCEPT:** If you've tried unsuccessfully to avoid, alter, and adapt, then acceptance is the final answer. Accept the imperfections in yourself and others. Try to find the silver lining in the experience. For example, being involved in roller derby can help you become a more tolerant person. Choosing acceptance can help you have a long and happy relationship with derby.

# MENTAL TOUGHNESS TIP #128
## Beware Of The Self-Fulfilling Prophecy

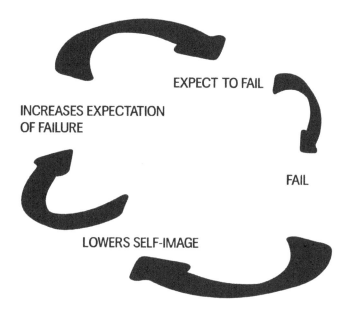

The Self-Fulfilling Prophecy is a scientifically proven phenomenon whereby expecting something to happen actually causes it to happen. As the vicious cycle of the negative self-fulfilling prophecy shows (above), when we expect failure and then fail, our self-image is lowered leading to a negative view of our abilities. This increases our expectation of future failure. A negative self-image effects our performance in many ways such as decreased motivation, effort, and commitment. What we believe is possible, or not possible, becomes reality.

The example that follows shows how negative predictions can create a cycle of reinforcement.

**Negative prediction:** *I can't stop the jammer.*
**Outcome:** The jammer skates by you untouched.
**Reinforced negative self-image:** *I knew it! I can't stop anyone. Why even try.*

This pattern can pull you further and further away from your goals and into a downward spiral of self-doubt and failure. Since our expectations have the power to make things happen, why not create an upward spiral based on positive predictions?

**Positive prediction:** *I can stop the jammer.*
**Outcome:** Maybe you stop them and maybe you don't. Don't beat yourself up. Instead, think, *I will stop them next time.* Eventually it will be true.
**Reinforced positive self-image:** *I knew I could stop the jammer! I can do it again!*

Continue to think positively and eventually your thoughts will manifest into reality.

*Some self-doubt is good because it helps maintain motivation and humility and prevents contentment and overconfidence.*

# MENTAL TOUGHNESS TIP #129
## Improve Your Attentional Focus

There are three elements of focus: selective attention, concentration, and attentional control. Selective attention is the ability to choose the most relevant thing to focus on. A skater needs to figure out which things they should pay attention to and which things are distractions. Concentration is the ability to sustain, or hold, one's attention to one thing over time.

Attention can be thought of like a flashlight beam. When you hold a flashlight, you can aim it here or there. That is selective attention. You can hold the beam of light for a long time in one direction or shift it between things rapidly. This is concentration. You can also move the flashlight closer or farther away from an object, lighting up a larger area or a smaller one. Our focus does this as well. Sometimes we have a broad focus, paying attention to many things at once. Sometimes our focus is very narrow, and we are tuned in to one detail. We can focus externally on what's going on around us and focus internally, illuminating what's going on in our mind and body.

Having attentional control means being able to mentally shift from external to internal, broad to narrow, and back as needed. Athletes need to be able to choose what is essential and stay focused on it for as long as necessary. The figure below shows the different dimensions of attention.

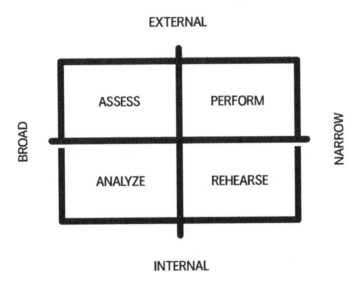

**Broad-external focus:** When we are assessing the situation.
**Broad-internal focus:** When we are analyzing our plan of attack.
**Narrow-internal focus:** When we are mentally rehearsing our next move.
**Narrow-external focus:** When we perform our move.

To improve your attentional control, use strategies for maintaining optimal arousal levels for performance. If you are too stressed or too relaxed your focus will suffer. These strategies include controlling respiration and heartbeat, managing catastrophic or upsetting thinking, and staying loose and ready in our muscles.

For help dealing with external distractions you can practice worst case scenarios. Practice with a "distraction partner" who tries to pull you off your game without contact. They can try trash talking (with agreed upon parameters), acting unexpectedly, or any other creative way they can act as a total distraction.

To improve internal attentional control. Recognize the negative self-talk or self-doubt that is distracting you and swap it for positive thoughts. You can develop rituals or protocols to trigger your concentration or certain feelings. One method is reciting motivational, instructional, and positive cue words such as:

*Fight*
*Fast*
*Strong*
*Fearless*

# MENTAL TOUGHNESS TIP #130
**Learn To Love Drills**

During practice you may dread certain drills, thinking, *Why do we have to do this for the millionth time?* The things we do over and over become our habits and our patterns. They become our reactions in high pressure situations because these brain pathways are the strongest. We can do them without thinking. This means when it is time to draw on that knowledge, your system can bypass the planning part of your brain, the Prefrontal Cortex (PFC). The movements will become "instinctual."

You may wonder why you try out all kinds of cool plays and strategies at practice, but it may take a year or more before they are spontaneously performed during a game. It is the same brain system at work. Practices are typically lower pressure than a game. The lack of intense stress will allow your PFC to remain online. You will be able to complete much more complicated and elaborate plays and strategies that require lots of thought. It is only through the process of intense repetition that you can make these a part of your regular game repertoire. The more similar the new actions are to ones you already perform in a game, the easier this process of translating skills from practice to competition will be. There is less of a synaptic leap.

# MENTAL TOUGHNESS TOOL
## BE RESTED: CHILD POSE

It is fundamental to notice the difference between rest and work, and effort and relaxation. In yoga, child pose is traditionally done on a mat, but you can also do this at a desk or table by gently resting your forehead on the back of your hands or stacked fists. There is a pressure point in between your eyebrows (sometimes called the Third Eye) that elicits a relaxation response.

Start on all fours, with elbows stacked over your wrists and your hips over your knees. Lower your hips back onto your heels. Knees can be together or apart. Arms can stretch out in front of you or lay gently at your sides. Rest your forehead on the mat. Hold for several breaths.

# MENTAL TOUGHNESS TIP #131
## See Challenges As Opportunities

When we meet a challenge or difficulty we can see it as a threat or we can see it as an opportunity to learn and grow. Part of how we assess challenges has to do with our world view which is based on our experiences and biology. However, we can change this up if it is not working for us. Think about your automatic reactions to difficulties. Do you run the opposite direction? Do you hide? Or do you say, "bring it on"? To succeed in sports, you must learn how to see challenging or difficult situations as opportunities.

In the counseling modality, Cognitive Behavioral Therapy, a person will identify beliefs that are problematic, unhelpful or irrational and transform them into helpful and rational ones. Let's learn how to transform unhelpful thinking.

1. How do you think about challenges? Write your thought or belief here:

_____

_____

2. How helpful or rational is this thought or belief?

| | | |
|---|---|---|
| Unhelpful | 1 2 3 4 5 6 7 8 9 10 | Helpful |
| Irrational | 1 2 3 4 5 6 7 8 9 10 | Rational |

3. How does this thought or belief influence your emotions, feelings, and actions?

_____

_____

4. What would be a more helpful, realistic way to think about challenges?

_____

_____

5. How will this new way of thinking influence your emotions, feelings, and actions?

_____

_____

When you can transform unhelpful or irrational thinking, you can change your emotions and actions.

# MENTAL TOUGHNESS TOOL
## BE POWERFUL: BE YOUR OWN SUPERHERO

Superheroes can be great role models, especially if we strive to embody their best traits. As the quote from the roller derby movie, *Whip It!* says, "Be your own hero." In so many comic book tales, someone is waiting for the hero to come save them. It is imperative that you know you can save yourself. You can become whatever you need to be to deal with any situation that comes your way.

On the next page, draw yourself as a superhero. Think of what kinds of skills, talents, and personality traits you want to embody. The next time you need some extra mental or physical strength, you can summon your inner superhero!

Here are a few powerful comic book superheroes to inspire you. Feel free to use non-comic heroes such as a fire fighter, surgeon, or marine.

**Captain Marvel:** Her powers include strength, durability, and the ability to absorb energy from lightning. She can also fly and shoot energy blasts from her hands.

**The Hulk:** When Bruce Banner transforms into the Hulk, he has unlimited strength, stamina and can heal himself. The Hulk is powered by pure rage.

**Phoenix:** With the Phoenix Force, she is one of the most powerful telepaths in the universe with unlimited mental powers.

**The Flash:** As the fastest man alive, he has the Speed Force and can run, think, and act faster than light. He can also move through time and matter.

**Wonder Woman:** She has the powers of the Greek gods and is a badass fighter. She also possesses the Lasso of Truth, a pair of indestructible bracelets, and a tiara so sharp it once cut Superman.

**Silver Surfer:** He wields the Power Cosmic, which gives him superhuman strength, endurance, and senses. He can also exceed the speed of light and navigate through interstellar space and hyperspace.

# MENTAL TOUGHNESS TIP #132
## Tone Your Vagus Nerve

Stephen Porges' Polyvagal Theory explains how our vagus system functions during times of stress. The vagus nerve is a cranial nerve that connects the brain to the body. It is named *vagus* because this means "wandering" in Latin. This long nerve wanders through organs in the face, neck, chest and abdomen. Among other things, it is responsible for the muscles of vocalization, facial muscles of expressivity, the muscles we use to gesture with our hands, and the autonomic digestion, respiration and heartrate functions of the parasympathetic nervous system. Polyvagal Theory posits we have a "tri-une" autonomic nervous system that approaches regulation with a hierarchy of three different systems when our body's neuroception system detects a threat to our safety. Most people know about our flight or fight stress response system, but according to this theory, we have three stress response systems. Polyvagal theory helps us understand these different circuits that are activated outside of our conscious will.

1. The *Social Engagement System* is the one we recruit first when we try to ask for help with facial expressions, hand gestures, or our voice.
2. If the Social Engagement System does not bring us back to a sense of safety, the next system, the *Sympathetic Nervous System* (SNS) is activated. This is our flight or fight response where we are signaled to flee. If fleeing isn't an option, the fight response takes over and we try to defend ourselves. The SNS mobilizes the torso and the limbs. If we are in this

state, we may not recognize it when people are trying to help us because they will appear as a threat. Constipation may be a problem.

3. If the activation of the SNS does not create safety or if the situation escalates, the *Parasympathetic Nervous System* (PNS) is activated. This is the freeze response. This primitive, immobilization response includes dissociation and shock. Issues relating to uncontrollable emptying of the digestive system is associated with the freeze response. Fear can literally scare the shit out of you.

Think about what your go-to response is to stress. Do you ask for help (through vocalizations or facial expressions)? Is your urge to run or hide? Is your impulse to fight or defend yourself? Do you freeze up, zone out, or shut down? Having this self-awareness will tell you where to focus when working toward a healthy *vagal tone*, the body's ability to respond successfully to stress. This work can prevent or de-escalate responses that are maladaptive and don't serve you. Read below to prevent or soothe the sympathetic nervous system's mobilization or flight or fight response:

**Prevention:**
- Activities that promote slow exhalations such as singing or playing wind instruments
- Minimize low, threatening tones in the environment
- Lots of healthy, social engagement

**Soothing:**
- Slow, deep breaths
- Focus on evidence of safety in your environment

- Relax the body (face, jaw, throat, neck, shoulders, hands, etc.)
- An extreme measure is to get the help of your inner dolphin by stimulating your body's "diving reflex." You can do this by putting your face in a bowl of ice water. The diving reflex lowers the heart rate when our face is cooled to enable our body to tolerate a lower level of oxygen. Consult a medical professional before you try this one.

To prevent or come out of a state of the parasympathetic nervous system's freeze or immobilization response, we need to mobilize:

**Prevention:**
- Movement including exercise, dance, or yoga
- Take part in activities that alert the system such as trying new things
- Mindfulness activities

**Mobilization:**
- Slap the leg muscles to wake them up
- Take three fast sips of air in through the nose, exhale out the mouth
- Grounding activities that involve the senses

Bonus tip: In 2012, researchers at the University of Boston School of Medicine discovered yoga's secret. It regulates the nervous system by increasing vagal tone. Practice yoga to harness the power of your vagus nerve and stay calm and cool in any high-pressure situation.

## MENTAL TOUGHNESS TIP #133
### Use The ABC's To Defeat Anxiety

Use the three steps, **A**ffirm, **B**reathe, and **C**hoose to deal with any bout of anxiety, stress, fear, or anger.

**AFFIRM:** Tell yourself something positive and helpful that is going to make you feel in control and confident.

*I can handle this.*

**BREATHE:** Take as many calming breaths as needed. Breathe slowly, evenly, and deeply. Allow the belly to expand and release. Breathe in and out through the nose.

**CHOOSE:** When your brain's Prefrontal Cortex is back online, you can make a mindful decision about what to do next.

# MENTAL TOUGHNESS TIP #134
## Have Pride

Sometimes it is difficult for us to talk about our achievements. We may feel like we are bragging or being boastful. But when we acknowledge what we've been able to do in the past, it will build our confidence to take on whatever the future holds. We will know that we have the capability to overcome obstacles, work hard, and meet challenges.

Complete the statement below with as many achievements as you can think of. They don't need to be roller derby accomplishments. When we recognize what we have been able to do in one area of life, we can use that awareness to give us the confidence to tackle another area.

**I am proud that I...**

1. _____

2. _____

3. _____

# MENTAL TOUGHNESS TOOL FOR TEAMS
## BE UNITED: MAKE A FOREST

This activity from the book, *Yoga Calm for Children, Educating Heart, Mind and Body,* is powerful for all ages. It develops trust and teamwork and only takes a couple of minutes. Consider doing this before games. It works well both on and off skates.

In a forest, groups of trees shield each other from getting knocked down by wind and link their roots for even greater support.

1. Make a circle, facing in, and standing a couple of feet apart.
2. Raise both arms and press your palms into the palms of your teammates on either side of you.
3. Lift your right leg up into Tree Pose (page 216 has directions for Tree Pose).
4. Press into one another's hands and feel the support you are both giving and receiving. Hold for five to eight breaths and then switch sides. A short discussion about the strength of a forest vs. individual trees makes this activity extra inspiring!

# MENTAL TOUGHNESS TIP #135
**Fuel Your Brain**

Try adding these types of foods to your regular diet to feel focused, calm, alert, and balanced. The foods on this list will give you stable mental and physical energy that won't dip out when you need it the most.

**Wholegrains:** Just like your body, the brain needs energy to work. The ability to concentrate and focus comes from an adequate, steady supply of energy in the form of glucose in our blood to the brain. Eating wholegrains releases glucose slowly into the bloodstream, keeping you mentally alert throughout the day. Choose "brown" wholegrain cereals, breads, rice, and pasta.

**Broccoli:** Broccoli is a great source of vitamin K and known to enhance cognitive function and improve brainpower. Broccoli is high in glucosinolates, which can slow the breakdown of the neurotransmitter, acetylcholine. Acetylcholine is needed to keep the central nervous system performing properly and to keep our brains and our memories sharp.

**Avocados:** Avocados and other "good fats" such as those found in oily fish, nuts, and seeds, are essential for optimum brain power and help alleviate stress and depression. Avocados are full of vitamin E, potassium, and omega 3 fatty acids. Without good fats, our blood sugar levels can drop, wrecking our energy and concentration. Go for guacamole or eat your avocado right out of the half-shell with salt and pepper.

**Seeds:** Seeds, especially pumpkin and sunflower seeds are high in the minerals magnesium, potassium, zinc, and selenium which are essential for focus and keeping us calm. Magnesium can help with insomnia, vital for those who can't sleep due to pre-game jitters.

**Eggs:** Eggs are packed full of amino acids, good fats, vitamins, and minerals. Eggs are high in vitamins B6, B12, and folic acid which are known to reduce levels of a compound called homocysteine in the blood. Elevated levels of homocysteine are associated with increased risk of stroke, cognitive impairment, and Alzheimer's disease. You can eat eggs hard boiled, scrambled or on whole grain bread. Get your eggs from free range chickens if possible.

**Dark chocolate:** Cocoa contains theobromine which contains tryptophan. Tryptophan is the basis for serotonin which elevates the mood. Look for choices that contain at least 70% cocoa solids.

**Black Currants:** Black currants may help reduce anxiety and stress. The vitamin C they contain increases mental agility, keeping your brain fast and flexible. You can also find this vital vitamin in red peppers and citrus fruits such as oranges.

Bonus tip: Keep your blood sugar balanced and sustain your brain boost by eating meals and snacks that are low on the glycemic index. One way to do this is by combining proteins and carbohydrates together. This will slow the rate sugar is released into the blood. Try eating an apple along with your seeds.

# MENTAL TOUGHNESS TIP #136
## Fill Your Mind With Positive Imagery

Visualize means to form a mental image of or see pictures in your mind. We all know we can see with our eyes, but we can also see with our mind. The mind can imagine or visualize, and the body can't tell if we are seeing something with our mind or with our eyes. Have you ever had a nightmare where you wake up and your body is sweating and your heart is racing? This is an example of how a picture in your mind can affect your body. That's why it is very necessary to fill your mind with positive, helpful images. Guided meditations are a way to do this.

### Confidence Boosting Guided Meditation
(Adapted from *A Guided Meditation to Help Quiet Self-Doubt and Boost Confidence* by Rebekah Borucki.)

Take a comfortable seat, sitting up straight and tall, bringing your focus to your breath, not trying to change your breath, but just noticing each inhalation and exhalation. Allowing your belly to slowly rise and fall with each breath. Breathing in and out several times as you notice tension starting to leave your mind and body.
This meditation is about building your confidence. Just by spending this time in meditation you are saying to yourself, *You matter*. The way we treat ourselves affects how others treat us, so it is imperative to feel good about yourself. Accept all the good and not so good parts about you.

Repeat this mantra three times to yourself:
*Even though I might not like every part of me,
I love who I am.*

Imagine a warm light inside your belly. Imagine it expanding and contracting with every inhale and exhale. With every inhale the light grows brighter and bigger, filling every part of you. Feel the light grow larger and warmer. Exhale and release all tension. Inhale and feel the light filling you all the way up. This warm light is an expression of your inner light. A light that exudes confidence. A light that brings all good things to you. When your light shines you appear more confident and you attract abundance and love and admiration and respect.

With every inhale allow that light to grow brighter. Exhale and release all tension. By releasing tension, we find ease in this body and we find comfort in this space. You appear at ease, you appear balanced, you attract respect. People look at you and wonder, "What have they got going on?" At this point in your meditation, you may be sitting up even taller, feeling stronger, maybe a smile is crossing your face. With every inhale you inhale peace and with every exhale you exhale confidence. The whole world feels your vibration, they feel the warmth of your light. They can see that you are an accomplished, confident, proud person, worthy of all the world has to offer you.

You attract all things with your inhales and your exhales because they allow you to shine bright. Inhale, exhale and release, inhale, exhale and let go. It is time to tell the world and yourself how worthy and capable you are. Every inhale is going to invite success and call the goodness to you. Now think of a word that means confident to you. It could be *strong, whole, powerful...* whatever comes to mind.

Inhale and say to yourself three times:
*I am _____, I deserve everything this world has to offer.*

By repeating this mantra, when you say these words again and again, your body starts to believe them, your words start to repeat them, they get into your thoughts, and then your actions become manifestations of those thoughts and words. So, you stand taller, you smile bigger, your voice gets louder, and people start to respond to this inner confidence you exude. Continue to follow your inhales and exhales, allowing your inner light to grow. When you are ready, you can slowly open your eyes, rise from meditation, and return to the world.

## MENTAL TOUGHNESS TOOL
### BE MINDFUL: ROLLER DERBY
### MINDFULNESS ACTIVITY II

At your next practice, do a roller derby activity that takes some paying attention to be successful. Choose something you are fairly confident in. Some ideas are jumps, transitions, falls, stops, and backwards skating. You will focus your attention completely on the task, being mindful, your head and body in the same place.

Your goals in completing this activity will be to:
1. Determine what you should be focusing on to be successful in this task.
2. Notice if your mind drifts away from the task and if it does, gently bring it back.
3. Be in the moment.
4. Be nonjudgmental (don't think of anything going on in your head or around you as being good or bad).

# MENTAL TOUGHNESS TIP #137
## BE A RISK TAKER

Our brain doesn't like us to take risks. It doesn't like unknowns. So, when the brain encounters one, it comes up with a prediction instead. The problem is this prediction comes from our amygdala, our primitive lizard brain. Since the lizard brain's job is to protect us from danger, it takes all the variables from the unknown situation and gives us a worst-case scenario answer. It tells us what will happen if everything goes wrong. This result is the one most people follow. Instead, ask yourself, "What if it works out?" This will trick your brain into giving you different options other than, *No way, too risky!* such as, *Hmmm, maybe I could do this.*

Risk taking provides the intrinsic and extrinsic rewards that occur when one accomplishes an amazing feat. But risk also provides the reward of flooding our brains with dopamine, the feel-good neurotransmitter. Studies on the brains of risk-takers reveal dopamine inhibiting receptors. This means those folks have even more dopamine levels in their brains than others, making risk especially rewarding.

Here are some things to consider when taking risks:
1. Would this risk be worth it to you even if you fail?
2. Is taking this risk in line with your highest values, with what is most important to you?
3. If you think the risk is too risky, what could you do to minimize the risk?
4. Will you regret not taking this risk?
5. What chance of success do you need to take a risk?
    0% chance of success
    25% chance of success

50% chance of success
75% chance of success
100% chance of success

Whether you succeed or fail, taking a risk will stretch you, giving you faith in your strength and abilities, and the confidence to do even more. Life doesn't come with guarantees. That can make it scary, but also incredibly fun. The parts of your life that are going to stand out aren't the times when you played it safe, they will be the times when you took a leap of faith, whether you won or not.

*"First you jump off the cliff
and you build wings on the way down."
-Ray Bradbury*

# MENTAL TOUGHNESS TIP #138
## Build An Internal Locus Of Control

Locus of Control is a theory of personality psychology developed by Julian Rotter in 1954. Locus of control is all about whether individuals believe they can control the events that affect them. Some people feel events are more controlled by external factors and some think they have more personal control over events. These different ways of thinking occur on a spectrum. At one end of the spectrum is what is called an external locus of control and at the other end is an internal locus of control. To get an idea of where you land on the spectrum, choose either "a" or "b" for each item below (these items are adapted from the full scale):

1. a) Many of the unhappy things in people's lives are partly due to bad luck.

   b) People's misfortunes result from the mistakes they make.

2. a) In the long run people get the respect they deserve in this world.

   b) Unfortunately, an individual's worth often passes unrecognized no matter how hard they try.

3. a) Becoming a success is a matter of hard work, luck has little or nothing to do with it.

   b) Success depends mainly on being in the right place at the right time.

4. a) When I make plans, I am almost certain I can make them work.

   b) It is not always wise to plan too far ahead because many things turn out to be a matter of good or bad fortune anyhow.

5. a) In the long run, the bad things that happen to us are balanced by the good ones.

b) Most misfortunes are the result of lack of ability, ignorance, laziness, or all three.

Give yourself one point for each of the following, (5 points possible):

1b   2a   3a   4a   5b

If you scored higher that may mean you think your destiny is in the hands of fate, luck, or powerful others. If you scored lower, you may believe your destiny is guided by your own efforts and involves such actions as hard work and personal decisions. One locus of control is not necessarily superior to the other. For sports, however, an internal locus of control may serve you better because it is related to decreased injury severity, resilience, perseverance, and grit in the face of adversity.

To shift to a more internal locus of control:
1. Recognize that you always have a choice. Making no choice is a choice in itself. By making no choice you are allowing other people or events to decide for you.
2. Set goals. By working toward your goals, you are controlling what happens in your life.
3. Develop your decision making and problem-solving skills. These skills can get you through tough situations.
4. Pay attention to your self-talk. If you catch yourself saying, "I have no choice," or "There's nothing I can do," remind yourself that you do have some control. Feeling like you have control over things gives you confidence.

# MENTAL TOUGHNESS TIP #139
## Connect Goals, Actions, and Values

Our roller derby goals are *what* we want to accomplish. Our values are *why* that goal matters to us. Our value-driven actions are *how* we are going to get there. Value-driven actions take us in the direction of our goals. Choosing the alternative—emotion-driven actions—may take us toward our goals, but they may not. Emotions are an inconsistent guide for our actions because they come and go. Whereas values are relatively stable.

As an example, say your goal is to hit harder and this is important to you because you value Success. Emotion-driven actions that could get in the way of achieving your goal include skipping practice when you're not in the mood and avoiding blocking someone who intimidates you. To achieve your goal, you would need to take actions that are aligned with Success such as attending practice regularly and taking on challenges. By sticking to your value-driven actions you will achieve your goal of hitting harder.

What is your derby goal?

_____

Why is this important to you? What is the related value(s)?

_____

Which emotion-driven actions could get in the way of achieving your goal?

_____

_____

What do you need to do more of or change to stay aligned with your value(s)? These are you value-driven actions.

_____

_____

Use the information above to fill in the worksheet on the following page.

*My goal is what I want to achieve.*
*My values are the reason this is important to me.*
*My value-driven actions will take me there.*

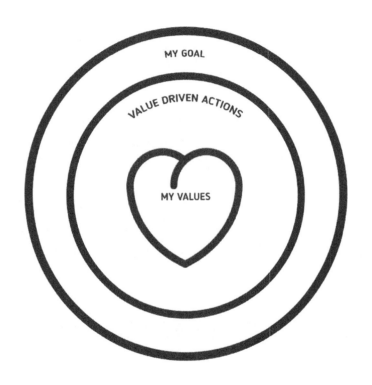

# MENTAL TOUGHNESS TIP #140
## Take Advantage Of Being Hot

The phenomenon of having "hot hands" or being "hot" is mainly known in the world of basketball. Much research has been done on whether a player who has just sunk a shot is more likely to sink the next. Players and fans believe in this phenomenon and chances are this "hot" player will be fed the ball for the next shot. It seems that having more opportunities to take shots would increase the likelihood of scoring again. But the data shows there is an "anti-hot hands" effect. A player who has just made a shot is more likely to miss on their second attempt, more so than chance would suggest. This could be due to several subtle factors including stepped up defense and overconfidence. But don't give up on being hot just yet. A recent paper by Richard B. Miller and Adam Surjurjo shows that players *can* ignite. These successful players do have statistically significant hot periods over the course of a game, just not necessarily hitting in the next consecutive attempt.

Now over to roller derby...can the success of a jammer in one jam influence their success in the next? The data above suggests we might not want to hand them the star again. But the beautiful complexity of humans means we can't predict with certainty what will happen. If a jammer feels confident and their team feels confident in them, then anything can happen. The latest research certainly shows that the phenomenon of being hot is a real thing across games. Therefore, if you are having a great game, it may be a good idea to jam (or block) more often.

# MENTAL TOUGHNESS TIP #141
## Take Credit Where Credit Is Due

In sports psychology, *attributions* are the explanations an athlete gives for the outcome of their performance. An attribution can be either negative or positive and is how an athlete explains their wins and losses. Using negative attributions to describe winning or losing decreases confidence and gives you expectations of failure in the future. Using positive attributions enhances your confidence, gives you expectations of success in the future, and will ultimately improve your performance.

Here are some different types of attributions from the book, *Bring Your 'A' Game* by Jennifer Etnier:

**Missed Opportunity:** This is a negative attribution for a win. A missed opportunity occurs when you have a great game and don't take credit for it. For example, say you have just done an amazing job at blocking, stopping the jammer every time. Afterwards someone says to you, "Amazing game! How do you do it?" If you respond by saying something such as, "I got lucky a lot of the time," you have just missed an opportunity for building confidence. This may seem like a modest, polite answer, but it doesn't give you any credit.

**Taking credit:** This is a positive attribution for a win. Don't forget about all the training, effort, and skill that went into your performance. It is okay to say something like, "Thanks! I've really been preparing for this game and I wanted to focus on taking more chances." This statement gives you credit for your part in the performance.

**Taking the blame:** This occurs when an athlete takes all the blame for their team's loss. This negative attribution typically occurs when the loss occurs in the final seconds of the game. Taking the blame for this kind of loss is unreasonable because there were other factors for the final score. Throughout the game there were many other opportunities for scoring, defending, making strategic decisions, and so on.

**Poor process:** This is a positive attribution for a loss. Instead of saying your less-than-stellar performance is due to being a sucky skater, attribute mistakes to poor performance processes. Performance processes are things a skater can work on such as re-entering the track legally or listening for your number being called to the box. In this way a skater can continue to set improvement goals and protect their confidence.

**Blaming others:** This is another negative attribution for a loss. This occurs when you blame the loss on things like dirty play by the opponents, bad ref calls, or your teammates. Blaming others can protect you from the pain of looking at your weaknesses. Blaming others does not give you the opportunity for learning and growth because none of the elements blamed are within a skater's control to change.

# MENTAL TOUGHNESS TIP #142
## Lose The Ego

An inflated ego can develop when people come to believe their superior talents make them superior people. Sometimes this happens because a skater receives this message from coaches, teammates, family, friends, or fans. A big ego causes a skater to look down on others.

Ego has no part in team sports, which is about standing shoulder to shoulder with teammates. Skaters who treat their teammates as inferior or expect special treatment destroy team harmony. A skater may end up alienating those they need to rely on to have their back.

An ego is a burden to bear. You will always perform the worst when you have a lot to lose. If you go into a jam with your ego on the line it can set you up to choke if you make a mistake.

To lose the ego, separate the performance from the person. An awesome performance doesn't mean one is an awesome person just like a failed performance doesn't mean one is a failure as a person. Here are some other tips:

1. Gratitude. Remember to show gratitude for your abilities.
2. Giving. Work on ways to make those around you better.
3. Thankfulness Be thankful for the opportunity to play this incredible sport.
4. Acknowledgment. Recognize the part your teammates play in your success.
5. Humility. Let your awesome performance speak for itself.

# MENTAL TOUGHNESS TOOL
## BE COMMITTED: BOW POSE

Wisdom says hitting the bullseye is the result of flying one hundred arrows. The bow and arrow have been used for warfare and used to hunt, providing food that sustains life. When cupid hits your heart with an arrow, will you fall in love? A much-admired bow is the rainbow. A rainbow can be seen after a rain when the sun emerges.

Lie on your belly. Make sure your knees remain hip width apart. Bend your knees and reach your hands back, taking hold of your shins, ankles, or feet. Inhale, lifting your head, heart, and legs. Pressing your feet into your hands creates the lift. If you are very flexible, you might be able to rock back and forth. Hold for three breaths.

When working in this pose, you may choose to consider the following:
1. How can I keep my aim straight?
2. How far should I bend?
3. Is there something I need to let go of?

# MENTAL TOUGHNESS TIP #143
## Take Opposite Actions

Think of a cat stuck in a tree. The cat wants out of the tree (his goal) but he doesn't take the steps he needs to get there. He gets caught up in his emotions (fear, mistrust, stubbornness) and thoughts (*Everyone needs to stay away from me! I can figure this out on my own!*) and does not see the bigger picture. The cat may do the opposite of what is in the service of his goal like scratch someone who is trying to help him or climb up higher. If he took *opposite actions*, he would do what he needed to get out of the tree even if that meant feeling fear or accepting help.

The ability to develop poise (being in control of your actions no matter what you are thinking or feeling), requires you to handle difficult situations and act in a way that is often the opposite of how you want to respond. You may have to move toward that which causes upsetting, uncomfortable, or negative emotions and thoughts rather than avoiding it. Athletes may discover the actions they need to take to be successful are the opposite of what their emotion's action urge tells them to do. A successful athlete can move forward into difficult, emotionally-charged situations. Taking these type of "approach" actions will help you to achieve your goals rather than provide short term relief from stress or difficult emotions.

In the chart on the following page are some examples of emotions, the emotion's action urge, and a helpful opposite action.

## Opposite Action Chart

| Emotion | Emotion's Action Urge | Opposite Action |
|---|---|---|
| Sad | Be alone, be quiet, not participate | Join in with others, get active |
| Angry | Yell, be hurtful, attack | Be extra kind, gently avoid |
| Frustrated | Give up, try too hard | Keep trying, slow down |
| Betrayed | Hurt or revenge | Forgiveness |
| Worthless | Be self-destructive | Treat yourself well |
| Fear | Avoidance, run away | Stay and do what is fearful |
| Shame | Hide | Be public |

# MENTAL TOUGHNESS TIP FOR TEAMS #144
**Pull Your Weight**

One of the things that can interfere with a team fulfilling their potential is something called The Ringelmann Effect. This group phenomenon was discovered and named after French agricultural engineer Maximilien Ringelmann. He measured the strength of individuals pulling on a rope and then added more people to the task. One would guess that if a single person pulled 100 lbs., then two people could pull 200 lbs., and so on. But that was not the case. The conclusion of this experiment was the more people there are in a group, the less effort each person will contribute. There is somehow a loss of motivation to give 100%.

When individuals in a group don't put forth 100% effort, sports psychologists call this *social loafing*. Some skaters may not give everything they've got because they feel like their teammates are handling it. This is especially true when skaters are grouped up with others at different skill levels. Skaters of lower levels may feel like they aren't really needed or don't have anything to contribute. Social loafing increases in larger groups. When there are only two of you on the track it becomes immediately apparent if one of you isn't pulling their weight. With four blockers, there are more places to hide. Here are some ways to maximize team motivation:

1. Group together with skaters of similar skill level during drills or scrimmages.
2. Make sure individual contributions can be identified and evaluated. When taking turns doing drills at practice ask someone who is on the sidelines to watch your performance and give you feedback afterwards.
3. Cross train in all positions at practice. Even though you may not typically jam in games, playing in this position at practice will help you gain an appreciation for every little assist you get.

# MENTAL TOUGHNESS TIP #145
## Be Resilient In The Face Of Adversity

Resiliency helps people go through stressful or adverse events in a way that allows them to emerge bigger, better, stronger, and wiser on the other side. Psychologist, Albert Ellis, created the ABC Model to help us understand our reactions to adversity. Our beliefs about the situation, not the event itself, are what causes us to be upset or act in certain ways.

'A' is the adversity or the stressful situation or event.
'B' is our belief or our explanation about why the situation happened.
'C' is the consequence or the feeling and behavior the belief causes.

*Adversity* ⟶ *Belief* ⟶ *Consequence*

Sometimes our beliefs about the situation or event aren't accurate. They have developed because of our past experiences but may not apply to the current reality. The feelings and actions that come because of our beliefs can undermine our ability to respond in a resilient way. If we can begin to uncover our faulty or unhelpful beliefs, this can lead to actions that will support achieving our goals.

In the book, *The Resilience Factor*, authors Karen Reivich and Andrew Shatte' developed a useful tool for identifying some common universal beliefs associated with negative emotional consequences (anger, sadness, anxiety/fear, guilt, and embarrassment).

### Common Belief-Consequence Connections

Violation of our rights..............................Anger

Actual loss or loss of self-worth...............Sadness

Future threat.................................Fear, Anxiety

Violation of another's rights........................Guilt

Loss of standing with others.........Embarrassment

You can work backwards by using the emotion you are feeling to uncover your beliefs. For example, if you are feeling guilt, you may believe you have violated another's rights. This belief may be faulty or unhelpful to your performance. You can use Socratic-style questioning to challenge any faulty or unhelpful beliefs. This will decrease your experience of the negative emotional consequences.

1. What is the evidence for and against this being true?
2. Is there another way to look at this?
3. What is the worst, best, bearable, and most realistic outcomes?
4. What would happen if I no longer held onto this belief?
5. If my best friend were in the same situation, what would I tell them?

# MENTAL TOUGHNESS TIP #146
## Deal With Disappointment

Sports can help individuals develop character by allowing them the opportunity to learn how to deal with disappointment. There are many chances for experiencing disappointment in roller derby. Here are a few of them:
- Not getting selected for the Allstar Team
- Failing to pass your minimum skills test
- Getting injured right before a game

In the book, *Foundations of Sport and Exercise Psychology*, social skills, independence, and hope are all mentioned as traits that can strengthen the ability to deal with disappointment. Social skills mean having the support of friends and family and being able to communicate your needs and ask for help. Independence means knowing who you are and feeling like you have some control over your world. Hope is feeling like things will turn out alright in the end and believing your efforts will be rewarded.

Next time you are faced with disappointment:
1. Use your support system. Don't be afraid to ask for help if needed. Your family and friends are there for you.
2. Separate your identity from your results. Remind yourself you are more than just a derby skater. The disappointing event doesn't define you as a person.
3. Stay optimistic. Tell yourself things will be okay and then act as if this is true. This means planning your next steps and putting them into action. Remain flexible in your thinking. What is the most helpful, positive, realistic way to look at things?

Furthermore, it can help you to deal with disappointment if you value failure. We tend to showcase our successes and hide our failures. This is because failing can make us doubt our abilities, make us feel like we don't belong, or that we aren't worthwhile. Failure can lead to intense emotions such as embarrassment, shame, and fear. But failure is the stuff that successes are built from. Remain persistent despite failure. Failure is not final. Failures tell us what we need to do differently. They get us back on track with more fire in our bellies.

Share your failure stories with as much pride as you do your wins. Make sure your failure story ends with some sort of resiliency statement like, "I'm still going." Without failure we can't learn. Therefore, own the process, celebrate it, and share it so others can learn too.

There are only two kinds of skaters, those who fail and those who will. Ups and downs are natural and failure can't be avoided. Great athletes identify what they learned in defeat and begin to see how it helps them to higher levels. However, the best tip for dealing with disappointment might be to take yourself less seriously.

# MENTAL TOUGHNESS TIP #147
## Achieve Your Goals With Confidence

Having confidence that you can achieve your goals will help you make these big changes. Rate the following questions on a scale from 1 to 10, with 10 being the highest:

As of right now, how *important* is it for you to achieve your roller derby goals?

1  2  3  4  5  6  7  8  9  10

As of right now, how *confident* are you that you will achieve your roller derby goals?

1  2  3  4  5  6  7  8  9  10

As of right now, where are you in terms of *commitment* and taking real, actual steps toward achieving your roller derby goals?

1  2  3  4  5  6  7  8  9  10

If you rated yourself low on importance or commitment, then it is likely you did not select a roller derby goal that is aligned with your values (what is most important to you). If your importance and commitment are high, but your confidence is low, complete the following items to boost your confidence:

This is why I want to achieve my goal (If you don't have many good reasons, you need to rethink your goal):
1.
2.
3.

These are my strengths and abilities that will help me achieve my goal:
1.
2.
3.

These are my past successes related to my goal:
1.
2.
3.

Think of three things that will increase your confidence:
1.
2.
3.

Now rate your confidence again:
As of right now, how confident are you that you will achieve your roller derby goals?

1  2  3  4  5  6  7  8  9  10

Your confidence rating should have increased. Now you have a roller derby goal that is important to you, more confidence that you can achieve it, and are committed to doing what it takes to make it happen.

*(See page 133 for help setting your roller derby goal.)*

## MENTAL TOUGHNESS TIP #148
**Enjoy The Rush**

Extreme sports like roller derby provide many benefits including an increase in self-confidence, a sense of humility, enhanced fear management skills, and that prized adrenaline rush. In response to threat, stress, or excitement, the adrenal glands release the hormone adrenaline, also known as epinephrine, into the bloodstream. Adrenaline is responsible for our fight or flight stress response and triggers specific processes in the body that are designed to help us escape from danger. This surge of hormones happens within seconds which is why it is called a "rush." The effects of adrenaline in the body can last up to an hour after an adrenaline rush.

Overproduction of adrenaline, which is seen in individuals exposed to chronic stress, leads to many emotional and physical health problems. Adrenaline is a normal, healthy response to stressful situations when we have the coping mechanisms to return to homeostasis after the threat has passed. In small, useful, jet-fuel-bursts, adrenaline allows us to:
- Tap into extra strength
- Block our perception of pain
- Have heightened experiences (this is the good feeling "adrenaline junkies" seek)
- Boost our immune system

Adrenaline has been blamed for poor behavior such as yelling, trash talk, or fighting. It can be easy to lose control due to a loss of an ability to think clearly once our stress response kicks in. Those who work in extreme situations (e.g. fire fighters, military, surgeons) train to be able to perform well under the effects of an adrenaline rush, and you can too.

Athletes in extreme sports can become addicted to the adrenaline rush. A 2016 study on rock climbers found the athletes showed withdrawal symptoms consistent with substance abusers when they weren't climbing—cravings, inability to experience pleasure, and negative emotions.

Our system reacts the same way whether there is danger actually present. This makes it possible to use imaginal processes such as thinking about the excitement, danger, and thrill of roller derby to experience the effects of adrenaline. Whether in response to real or imaginal extreme sport situations, enjoy the benefits of your rush!

*(See page 104 for a basic mindfulness exercise that will help you begin to regulate your emotions and behavior.)*

# MENTAL TOUGHNESS TOOL
## BE POSITIVE: GUIDED MEDITATION FOR HAPPINESS

Ask yourself if you are having a good day. If you are having a good day, why is that? If you aren't having a good day, why? The more your happiness is dependent on external circumstances, the more unstable it will be. Your happiness will blow this way, or that, according to how your life is going.
- Coach is grumpy
- Can't find your favorite socks
- Your friend is skipping practice
- It is raining
- Store is out of your favorite snack
- Forgot your water bottle
- You didn't know practice time had changed

Rather than hanging your happiness on constantly shifting elements in your life, create stable joy from within. This kind of joy is always there inside of you.

Sit with your back straight and shoulders relaxed. Your eyes can be closed or the gaze softened.
Begin to breathe in and out through your nose. Focus on the sensation of your breath, just at the tip of your nose.
When you exhale, breathe out anything that doesn't serve you. Breathe out any frustrations, anger, fear, or worries that you may have. Breathe them out like a thick, dark smoke. Continue like this for as long as feels right. When you breathe in, breathe in a bright, white light. Breathe in this expansive, positive energy. Continue like this, breathing in light, for as long as you

need. Allow this white light to fill you completely, expanding out through every surface of your body. You are a radiant field of bright, white light.

When you are ready, you can rise from this meditation. Regular practice of this meditation will create a stable happiness within you.

# MENTAL TOUGHNESS TIP #149
## Burn The Boats

If you want to be successful, you must burn the boats. The concept of burning boats traces back to the 1519 story of Hernán Cortés. He led an expedition to Mexico with the goal of capturing a treasure said to be held there. When he got there, Cortés made history by destroying his ships. This sent a clear message to his men that there was no turning back. They would either need to win or they would perish. With no exit strategy in place, Cortés' men rallied behind their leader. Within two years, he succeeded in his conquest of the Aztec empire.

At its essence, burning boats represents a point of no return, a psychological commitment where you realize you have crossed a line that you can't cross back over. All your thoughts and efforts must be consumed with succeeding in this new reality.

Do you have a back-up plan if this whole derby thing doesn't work out? Is that safety net keeping you from putting in the effort, concentration, and commitment you need to really succeed at this sport? Once you have decided to do this, you must be willing to do it wholeheartedly. Don't allow fear and self-doubt to derail you. Don't dwell on the negative "what-ifs." Focus on the task at hand and the steps you need to take to be successful.

Safety nets and escape routes can protect you from pain and injury. But they can decrease your investment in the process. Once you have determined that this is what you want to do, burn the boats behind you and trust your inner voice to pursue your dreams. Don't look back!

# MENTAL TOUGHNESS TIP #150
**Savor The Peaks**

Roller derby isn't all sunny skies. Sometimes you must weather some storms. This is a hardcore, mentally and physically challenging sport. As such, you won't always feel good on your way to success. But when the peak moments do come, savor them completely.

# APPENDIX

## Solutions

Find the word, "DIFFICULT":

| F | U | D | I | U | F | F | D | D | L |
|---|---|---|---|---|---|---|---|---|---|
| T | U | I | U | U | U | C | D | F | C |
| I | F | F | L | C | T | U | L | D | F |
| C | I | F | C | I | C | T | U | T | F |
| T | L | I | L | I | U | F | D | L | L |
| F | C | C | L | C | L | F | L | U | F |
| I | L | U | F | U | U | F | C | D | L |
| U | L | L | U | L | D | D | T | L | T |
| T | D | T | I | L | D | U | I | T | I |
| D | L | T | I | F | I | L | L | U | U |

Spot the "b":

dddddd
dddddd
ddddbd

ddddddd
ddddddd
dbddddd
ddddddd

dddddddd
ddddddd**b**d
dddddddd
dddddddd
dddddddd

ddddddddddd
ddddddddddd
d**b**dddddddddd
ddddddddddd
ddddddddddd
ddddddddddd

d d d d d d d d d d d d d d
d d d d d d d d d d d d d d
d d d d d d d d d d d d d d
d d d d d d d d d d d d d d
d d d d d d d d d b d d d d d
d d d d d d d d d d d d d d
d d d d d d d d d d d d d d

**How many squares in this picture?**

Answer: 10

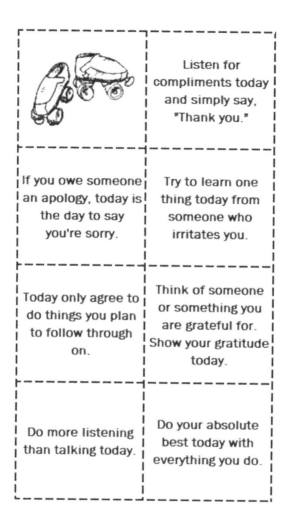

| | Listen for compliments today and simply say, "Thank you." |
|---|---|
| If you owe someone an apology, today is the day to say you're sorry. | Try to learn one thing today from someone who irritates you. |
| Today only agree to do things you plan to follow through on. | Think of someone or something you are grateful for. Show your gratitude today. |
| Do more listening than talking today. | Do your absolute best today with everything you do. |

| For one whole day, be honest. Don't lie or exaggerate. | Don't speak negatively about others today. If friends start to gossip, walk away. |
| --- | --- |
| Instead of taking yourself too seriously, laugh at yourself if you make a mistake today. | Let the other person be right today. |
| Look for someone who needs some help today and offer to help them. | Think of someone you offended recently. Surprise them by treating unkindness with kindness. |
| If you see somebody doing or saying something you don't agree with today, speak up! | |

F N P V D

B A K O E

T H W F M

X F R T O

A D V S X

N C B K F

K E P M A

A R D L G

S O G P B

T K U Z L

O E A N C

G D B K E

P S M A R

U A X S O

S N C T K

V S X P E

E A N C B

D B K E P

S M A R D

A X S O G

# REFERENCES

Much of the material for this book was shamelessly plundered from the following resources. Please investigate them for further understanding.

(2018, August). Retrieved from Psychology Tools: Psychologytools.com

(2018, August). Retrieved from Brainworks Train Your Mind: www.brainworksneurotherapy.com

(2018, August). Retrieved from Peak Performance Sports: Mental Training for a Competitive Edge: www.peaksports.com

(2018). Retrieved from The Peak Performance Center: http://thepeakperformancecenter.com/development-series/skill-builder/personal-effectiveness/goal-setting/setting-goals/performance/

*A Guided Meditation to Help Quiet Self-Doubt and Boost Confidence*. (2017, May 18). Retrieved from Health: https://www.health.com/fitness/self-confidence-meditation

Avila, E. (2016, July 6). *High Powered Performance: Hyrdration tips for all athletes*. Retrieved from

Stack: http://www.stack.com/a/high-powered-performance-hydration-tips-for-all-athletes

Benton, D. e. (2016). Minor degree of hypohydration adversely influences cognition: a mediator analysis. *The American Journal of Clinical Nutrition*.

*Breathwork Basics: Kapalabhati and Breath of Fire.* (n.d.). Retrieved from Five Pillars Yoga: http://www.fivepillarsyoga.com/breathwork-basics-kapalabhati-breath-of-fire/

Buddelmeyer, H., & Powdthavee, N. (2015). Can having internal locus of control insure against negative shocks? Psychological evidence from panel data. *Journal of Economic and Behavioral Organization*, 88-109.

Burrowes, B. (n.d.). *How Planing a Seed Can Change Your Life*. Retrieved from Tiny Buddha: https://tinybuddha.com/blog/plant-a-seed-change-your-life/

Bystritsky, A., Khalsa, S., & et, al. (2013). Current Diagnosis and Treatment of Anxiety Disorders. *Pharmacy and Therapeutics*, 41-44.

Clark, F. J., & et al. (2015). Vision Training Methods for Sports Concussion MItigation and Management.

*Journal of Visualized Experiments*.

Clear, J. (2014, April 10). *How Long Does It Actually Take to Form a New Habit (Backed by Science)*. Retrieved from Huffington Post: https://www.huffingtonpost.com/james-clear/forming-new-habits_b_5104807.html

Conefrey, G., & Bruinvels, G. (2018, October). Fitrwoman App.

*CTE Resources: Subconcussive Impacts*. (n.d.). Retrieved from Consussion Legacy Foundation: https://concussionfoundation.org/CTE-resources/subconcussive-impacts

Dweck, C. S. (2014, September 12). The Power of Yet. TedX Talks.

Edwards, V. (n.d.). *Body Language in Sports*. Retrieved from Huffington Post: https://www.huffingtonpost.com/vanessa-van-edwards/body-language-in-sports_b_4110590.html

Epstein, D. (2013). *The Sports Gene: Inside the Science of Extraordinary Athletic Performance.*

Fajkis, M. M. (2013, December 17). *Stressed: Overwhelmed? Take a yogic power nap.*

Retrieved from Elephant Journal: https://www.elephantjournal.com/2013/12/stressed-overwhelmed-take-a-yogic-power-nap/

Gillen, L., & Gillen, J. (2008). *Yoga Calm For Children: Educating Heart, Mind, and Body.* Three Pebble Press, LLC.

Good, S. (n.d.). *Living the creative life*. Retrieved from Good Life Coaching: http://www.goodlifecoaching.com/CreativeLife41.html

Gregory, S. (2010, October 22). *Can Football Finally Tackle Its Injury Problem?* Retrieved from Time: http://content.time.com/time/nation/article/0,8599,2027053,00.html

Hardavella, G. (2017). How to give and receive feedback effectively. *Breathe*, 327-333.

*Heartmath* . (n.d.). Retrieved from Heartmath : https://www.heartmath.com/

Heirene, R. M., & et al. (2016). Addiction in Extreme Sports: An exploration of withdrawal states in rock climbers. *Journal of Behavioral Addition*, 332-341.

Holzel, B., & et al. (2011). Mindfulness practice leads to

increases in regional brain gray matter density. *Psychiatry Research Neuroimaging*, 36-43.

*Honey Locust*. (n.d.). Retrieved from Honey Locust Sangha: http://honeylocustsangha.weebly.com/

Hughes, S. (2014, July 15). *Foods to Fuel the Brain*. Retrieved from Top Universities: https://www.topuniversities.com/blog/foods-fuel-brain

Kumar, M., & Mukesh, J. (2009). Study on the effect of Pranakarshan Pranayama and Yoga Nidra on Alpha EEG and GSR. *Indian Journal of Traditional Knowledge*, 453-454.

Landesman, P. (Director). (2015). *Concussion* [Motion Picture].

Lewin, J. (2017, July 7). *10 foods to boost your brainpower*. Retrieved from Good Food: https://www.bbcgoodfood.com/howto/guide/10-foods-boost-your-brainpower

Lewin, J. (2017, July 25). *Spotlight on low-GI*. Retrieved from Good Food: https://www.bbcgoodfood.com/howto/guide/spotlight-low-gi

Lindseth, P. (2013). Effects of hydration on cognitive

function of pilots. *Military Medicine*, 792-798.

McCraty, R., & et al. (2014). Cardiac coherence, self-regulation, autonomic stability, and psychosocial well-being. *Frontiers in Psychology*.

McCrory, P., & et al. (n.d.). *Consensus statement on concussions in sport—the 5th international conference on concussions in sport held in Berlin, October 2016*. Retrieved from British Journal of Sports Medicine: https://bjsm.bmj.com/content/51/11/838

McHugh, B. S., & et al. (2014). Aversice Predicdtion Error Signals in the Amygdala. *The Journal of Neuroscience*, 9024-9023.

McNamee, M., Partridge, B., & Anderson, L. (2015). Concussion in Sport: Conceptual and Ethical Issues. *Kinesiology Review*, 190-202.

Mez, J., Daneshvar, D., & Kiernan, P. (2017). Clinicopathological Evaluation of Chronic Traumatic Encephalopathy in Players of American Football. *Journal of American Medical Association*, 360-370.

Miller, J., & Sanjurjo, A. (2015). Surprised by the Gambler's and Hot Hand Fallacies? A Truth in the Law of Small Numbers. *EGIER Working Paper No.*

*552*, Miller, Joshua B. and Sanjurjo, Adam, Surprised by the Gambler's and Hot Hand Fallac Available at SSRN: https://ssrn.com/abstract=2627354 or http://dx.doi.org/10.213.

Miller, R. (2015). *The iRest Program for Healing PTSD: A Proven-Effective Approach to Using Yoga Nidra Meditation and Deep Relaxation Techniques to Overcome Trauma.* New Harbinger Publications.

Pargman, D., & Lunt, S. (2009). The relationship of self-concept and locus of control to the severity of injury in freshmen collegiate football players. *Sports Medicine, Training and Rehabilitation*, 203-208.

Park, A. (2008, December 30). *Why we take risks--it's the dopamine*. Retrieved from Time: http://content.time.com/time/health/article/0,8599,1869106,00.html

Podlog, L. W. (2012). Pain and Performance. *The Handbook of Sport and Performance Psychology*, 618-834. Retrieved from https://www.researchgate.net/publication/306438468_Heil_J_Podlog_L_2012_Pain_and_Performance_In_S_Murphy_Ed_The_Oxford_handbook_of_sport_and_performance_psychology_pp_6

Porges, S. W. (2011). *The Polyvagal Theory: Neurophysiological Foundations of Emotions, Attachment, Communication, and Self-regulation.* W. W. Norton & Company.

*Practice Better Than You Compete.* (n.d.). Retrieved from Believe Perform: https://believeperform.com/performance/practice-better-than-you-compete/

Rabideau, S. R. (005, October). *Effects of Achievement Motivation on Behavior.* Retrieved from Personality Research: http://www.personalityresearch.org/papers/rabideau.html

*Relax Kids.* (n.d.). Retrieved from Relax Kids: https://www.relaxkids.com/

Resnick, B. (2018, April 30). *What a lifetime of playing football can do to the human brain.* Retrieved from Vox: https://www.vox.com/science-and-health/2018/2/2/16956440/concussion-symptoms-cte-football-nfl-brain-damage-youth

Robbins, M. (2017). *The 5 Second Rule.* Savio Republic: Simon & Schuster.

Robert Weinberg, D. G. (2006). *Foundations of Sport and Exercise Psychology 4th Edition.* Human Kinetics.

Robinson, O., & et al. (2013). Stress increases aversive prediction error signals in the ventral striatum. *Proceedings of the National Academy of Sciences of the United States of America*.

Ruani, A. (n.d.). *4 Remarkable Ways Music Can Enhance Athletic Performance*. Retrieved from The Health Sciences Academy: https://thehealthsciencesacademy.org/health-tips/music-can-enhance-athletic-performance/

Schafer, T., Sedlmeier, P., Stadtler, C., & Huron, D. (2013). The Psychological Functions of Music Listening. *Frontiers in Psychology*.

Sentis. (2012, November 6). *Neuroplasticity*. Retrieved from YouTube: https://www.youtube.com/watch?v=ELpfYCZa87g

Sharot, T. (2018, June 15). *Why Stressed Minds Are More Decisive*. Retrieved from BBC: http://www.bbc.com/future/story/20180613-why-stressed-minds-are-better-at-processing-things

Singh, G., & et al. (2010). Yoga Nidra: a deep mental

relaxation approach. *British Journal of Sports Medicine*.

Spencer, S. (2014, April 6). *Are elite athletes born or made?* Retrieved from CBS News: www.cbsnews.com are elite athletes born or made

Stamm, J. M., & et al. (2015). Age of first exposure to football and later-life cognitive imipairment in former NFL players. *Neurology*.

Stretter, C., Gerbarg, P., Saper, R., Ciraulo, D., & Brown, R. (2012). Effects of yoga on the autonomic nervous system, gamma-aminobutyric-acid, and allostasis in epilepsy, depression, and post-traumatic stress disorder. *Medical Hypothesis*, 571-579.

Sullivan, R. (2017, April 28). *How We Use External Focus and Feedback To Train Our Athletes*. Retrieved from Florida Baseball Ranch: http://floridabaseballranch.com/blog/how-we-use-external-focus-and-feedback-to-train-our-athletes-part-1/

Taylor, D. J. (2017, December 6). *3 Essential MIndsets for Atletic Success*. Retrieved from Huffington Post: https://www.huffingtonpost.com/dr-jim-taylor/3-essential-mindsets-for_b_6142880.html

*The 25 Most Powerful Superheroes of All Time*. (n.d.). Retrieved from List 25: https://list25.com/the-25-most-powerful-superheroes-of-all-time/

*The Art of Now: Six Steps for Living in the Moment*. (n.d.). Retrieved from Psychology Today: https://www.psychologytoday.com/us/articles/200811/the-art-now-six-steps-living-in-the-moment

*The Diving Reflex*. (n.d.). Retrieved from Breatheology: https://www.breatheology.com/mammalian-dive-response/

*Thich Nhat Hanh*. (n.d.). Retrieved from Plum Village: https://plumvillage.org/about/thich-nhat-hanh/

Thompson, J. (n.d.). Elevate Your Game. In J. Thompson, *Elevate Your Game.* Positive Coaching Alliance.

*To Be Successful, Burn Your Boats*. (2017, September 18). Retrieved from Success: https://www.success.com/to-be-successful-burn-your-boats/

Torrens, K. (2018, July 11). *How much water should I drink in a day?* Retrieved from Good Food: https://www.bbcgoodfood.com/howto/guide/how-much-water-should-i-drink-day

*Tracking: Saccades*. (n.d.). Retrieved from Eye Can Learn: http://eyecanlearn.com/tracking/saccades/

*Via Instititute on Character*. (2018). Retrieved from Via Institute on Character : www.viacharacter.org

Vickers, J. (2016). Origins and Issues in Quiet Eye Research. *Current Issues in Sport Science*, 1-11.

Vine, S. J. (2017). Success is in the eye of the beholder: A Special Issue on the Quiet Eye. *European Journal of Sport Science*.

Weinberg, R., & et al. (2013). Playing Through Pain and Injury: Psychosocial Considerations. *Journal of Clinical Sport Psychology*, 41-59.

Weitz, N. (2014). *The Ultimate Mental Toughness Guide: Roller Derby.* San Bernadino: Createspace.

Weitz, N. (2016). *The Ultimate Mental Toughness Guide: Junior Roller Derby.* San Bernadino: Createspace.

WFTDA. (2018). *Risk Management Guidelines.*

*What is Yoga*. (n.d.). Retrieved from Yoga Alliance: https://www.yogaalliance.org/About_Yoga/What_is_Yoga

Williams, J. M. (2006). *Applied Sport Psychology.* McGraw Hill Higher Education.

*Yoga Nidra—the "rest" component in sport.* (n.d.). Retrieved from Sportsyoga: http://sportsyoga.ie/index.php/yoga-nidra-the-rest-component-in-sport/

## ABOUT THE AUTHOR

Naomi Sweetart Weitz is a Licensed Mental Health Counselor, Certified in Sports and Fitness Psychology, a Licensed Yoga Calm Trainer, and Registered Yoga Teacher. She has been involved in roller derby since 2006, founding Spokannibals Roller Derby in 2010.

Made in the USA
Coppell, TX
05 December 2019